INTRODUCTION

Welcome to "Starting An Etsy Business: A How To Guide"!

Are you ready to turn your passion into profit and embark on an exciting journey of creativity and entrepreneurship? If so, you've come to the right place. In this comprehensive guide, I'll take you by the hand and show you everything you need to know to launch, grow, and thrive as an Etsy seller. Welcome to the remarkable world of Etsy entrepreneurship—a world where creativity knows no bounds, where your artistic talents can become a thriving source of income, and where dreams of turning your passions into profits can be realized. Whether you're an artist, a craftsperson, a vintage collector, or a digital creator, this book is your compass on the exciting journey of starting and growing a profitable Etsy business.

Starting a business can be daunting, but it's also incredibly rewarding. Whether you're a craft enthusiast, an artist, or a vintage collector, Etsy provides a unique platform to showcase your talents and connect with millions of buyers around the world. With the right guidance and strategies, you can transform your dreams into a thriving business that brings joy to both you and your customers.

I'll offer you some insights, some tools, and the occasional reality check to help you on your way. But there are a few things I can't do.

I don't know you personally, or you skills or products. I don't know your history in the retail industry, or your familiarity with online processes or computers. I don't know where you live, or how much you're willing to work to make this happen. For all of those reasons, the information here is general. It's agnostic. It applies to most business types, but possibly not all. The guidance around laws and taxes, for example, will always need to be confirmed by a professional familiar with your offering, your area, and your country. Please understand that if I encourage you to get professional advice on something, that's my best advice!

But where do you begin? That's where "Starting An Etsy Business" comes in. Drawing on years of experience and expertise, I and many of my colleagues have compiled a wealth of invaluable insights, practical advice, and actionable tips to help you navigate the exciting world of Etsy entrepreneurship with confidence and clarity.

From setting up your shop and optimizing your listings to marketing your products and providing top-notch customer service, we'll walk you through every step of the journey. You'll learn how to identify your niche, create compelling product descriptions and photography, master the art of pricing and shipping, and much more.

Opening an Etsy business offers a myriad of opportunities for individuals seeking to turn their creative passions into profitable ventures and lucrative side hustles. Here are several compelling reasons people tell me they want to start an Etsy business:

At its heart, Etsy celebrates the art of creating. It's a platform that honors the dedication, skill, and love that go into making something by hand. Whether you're an artist, crafter, designer, collector, or maker, Etsy offers a space to bring your creative visions to life and share them with the world.

Etsy boasts millions of buyers actively searching for distinctive, one-of-a-kind items. These buyers appreciate the personal touch that comes with handmade or vintage goods. By setting up shop on Etsy, you gain access to a vast and diverse audience, all eager to discover and support your craft.

Navigating the world of online selling can be daunting, but Etsy's user-friendly platform simplifies the process. You don't need to be a tech wizard to set up your shop and start selling. With a few easy steps, you can showcase your creations to the world.

Beyond just a marketplace, Etsy is a community that fosters collaboration and offers resources to help you succeed. Forums, webinars, and seller education resources are readily available to assist you in building your business acumen.

One of the most appealing aspects of running an Etsy business is the flexibility it offers. Entrepreneurs have the freedom to set their own schedule, work from anywhere, and pursue their passions on their own terms. This flexibility allows for a better work-life balance and the ability to prioritize personal and family commitments than most side hustles and part time jobs.

Unlike traditional brick-and-mortar businesses, starting an Etsy shop requires minimal investment and overhead costs. With a low barrier to entry, virtually anyone with a creative idea and a computer can launch a successful Etsy business, making entrepreneurship accessible to people from all walks of life.

Etsy's global marketplace connects sellers with millions of potential customers worldwide. This vast reach provides unparalleled opportunities for exposure and sales, allowing entrepreneurs to tap into new markets and expand their customer base far beyond their local community.

Etsy fosters a vibrant and supportive community of like-minded creatives who share tips, advice, and encouragement. Sellers have access to forums, groups, and resources where they can connect with fellow entrepreneurs, collaborate on projects, and seek guidance on various aspects of running their businesses.

Running an Etsy business empowers individuals to take control of their financial destiny and pursue their entrepreneurial dreams. By building a successful business from the ground up, entrepreneurs can experience a sense of pride, accomplishment, and independence that comes from creating something of their own. It's a great way to learn whether entrepreneurship is for you, with minimal risk of financial loss.

Etsy offers endless opportunities for growth and expansion. As entrepreneurs gain experience and build their brand reputation, they can explore new product lines, experiment with different marketing strategies, and scale their businesses to new heights. Many even open brick and mortar locations.

Many Etsy sellers are passionate about sustainability, ethical sourcing, and supporting local communities. By selling handmade, vintage, or unique items, entrepreneurs can make a positive impact on the environment, support artisans and small businesses, and contribute to a more sustainable and equitable economy.

Overall, opening an Etsy business is a journey filled with optimism, creativity, and hard work. It's an opportunity to pursue your passions, connect with customers around the world, and build a business that reflects your values and vision.

But "Etsy Entrepreneur" isn't just about the nuts and bolts of running a business—it's also about embracing the entrepreneurial mindset and cultivating the determination, resilience, and creativity needed to succeed in today's competitive marketplace. With thought-provoking exercises, and practical strategies for overcoming challenges and setbacks, this book will empower you to unleash your full potential and achieve your goals.

So, if you're ready to take the leap and pursue your passion for crafting, creating, or curating, dive into "Starting An Etsy Business" and let's embark on this exciting journey together. Your dream business awaits—let's make it a reality!

CHAPTER 1: FINDING YOUR NICHE

Are you a creative soul with a passion for making, or curating, and selling beautiful things? Do you dream of turning your creativity into a profitable venture? Well, you're in the right place! Welcome to the world of starting a profitable Etsy business. Because Etsy is an online marketplace with a huge built-in customer base – nearly 100 million active buyers in 234 countries, it can be an ideal platform to sell your wares. In this exciting journey, I'll guide you through every step, starting with the crucial task of finding your niche.

Joining Etsy: Your Creative Journey Begins

Joining the Etsy marketplace is your ticket to sharing your unique creations with the world and making a living doing what you love. Before you open a shop, learn your way around. Let's discuss what to look for.

Start by opening your preferred web browser and typing in "www.etsy.com." Hit enter, and you'll be greeted by the colorful and welcoming world of Etsy. Etsy's homepage is a treasure trove of inspiration. Take your time to explore the featured items, shops, and trending collections. This will give you a feel for the diverse range of products and styles on Etsy. These shops will be your neighbors, just as if they had storefronts next to yours on a busy street in your town.

If you have a specific product or category in mind, use the search bar at the top of the page. Type in keywords related to what you want to sell or find, and Etsy will show you relevant results. This will give you lots of ideas about the possibilities of what is selling, as well as the talents you may have that you haven't realized you can monetize!

Etsy categorizes its products into various sections. You can navigate through these categories to discover different niches and get ideas for your own shop. Take a lot of notes about what you do and don't like, and use them to craft your brand.

Explore the Seller Forums! Etsy hosts a bustling community of sellers, and joining the seller forums is a fantastic way to connect with like-minded individuals. You can find these forums by clicking on "Community" at the top of the Etsy homepage and selecting "Seller Forums." Here, you can ask questions, share experiences, and gain valuable insights from experienced sellers. Most of these sellers are happy to work with other sellers – it's not a competitive mindset. With each person creating unique work, there is very little head to head competition. The exception is if you are selling drop-shipped products, in which case other sellers may be selling the exact same product.

Embrace the learning curve. Even if you're a regular Etsy shopper, there are factors and processes to being an Etsy seller that will take time to learn and navigate. Learning will be both fun and frustrating. Remember that every successful Etsy seller started somewhere. It's okay to make mistakes and learn as you go. For most sellers it takes 9 months to 1 year to become fully comfortable running their shop. Embrace the process, and don't be afraid to ask for help when you need it. Other sellers, and Etsy employees are always available to help.

Etsy provides a plethora of resources to help you succeed. Explore their "Seller Handbook" for tips on running a successful shop, and don't forget to check out their blog for the latest updates and advice.

What's A Niche? And Why Do I Need One?

A product niche on Etsy refers to a specific and focused market segment within the larger Etsy marketplace. For example, within the broader category of "jewelry" on Etsy, there are numerous product niches, such as "handmade gemstone jewelry," "vintage-inspired bridal jewelry," or "geometric minimalist jewelry." Each of these niches targets a specific audience and offers unique products that cater to their preferences.

You want to choose a niche that is characterized by a distinct set of products or product categories, and a target audience with unique preferences. This increases the likelihood your buyers will find you when they are ready to buy.

Key characteristics of a product niche on Etsy may include:

Specialized Products: Sellers within a niche offer products that are distinct and cater to a specific need, interest, or passion.

Targeted Audience: Niche sellers focus their marketing efforts on a particular group of buyers who share common interests, preferences, or hobbies related to the niche. You want to get specific here! Examples include second wedding brides, classical guitarists, or H-O scale train enthusiasts.

Unique Style or Theme: Niche products often have a consistent style, theme, or design aesthetic that appeals to the niche's target audience. Consider these examples: cottage core, Craftsman, steampunk, or grunge.

Limited Competition: In a niche, there may be fewer sellers offering similar products compared to broader categories, allowing for reduced competition and increased visibility. Shoppers on Etsy share their finds with friends and loved ones, and they also share on their themed Pinterest boards! When you resonate within your niche, you can receive amplification of your posts.

Passionate Community: Niche markets may have a dedicated and engaged community of buyers and sellers who are enthusiastic about the products and the niche itself.

Ultimately, identifying and successfully operating within a product niche on Etsy can lead to a more focused and effective approach to selling. It allows sellers to tailor their products and marketing efforts to a specific group of buyers with shared interests.

Start with What You Love. The first rule of thumb when searching for your niche is to follow your heart. What are you passionate about? What do you love creating or collecting? Whether it's handcrafted jewelry, personalized artwork, vintage clothing, or unique home decor, your passion can become the driving force behind your Etsy business. Get specific. What do you love? Why do you love it? What makes you love creating or curating it? The more you can articulate your passion, the easier it will be to describe, price, and sell your products.

Take some time to write a few paragraphs about your passion and desired product set. Your words of enthusiasm will start to help you shape your keyword list for describing your brand and your products. Describe how you began your journey in your creative life, or some work you're really proud of. These notes will be your reference when you start filling your shop and writing product titles and descriptions.

Analyze Your Skills. Take stock of your expertise. What is your strongest creative skill? Maybe you're a whiz with a sewing machine, an expert in woodworking, or a talented painter. Perhaps you make creative spreadsheets, or amazing woodworking plans. Your skills can be an asset in finding your niche because they provide you with a competitive advantage.

You may want to begin you Etsy experience with one group of products, and add over time. You'll be most successful if you're not trying to learn a new craft or trade while you're trying to set up your shop.

Research the Competition. Once you have a few ideas in mind, it's essential to research your potential competitors within those niches. What are they selling? What sets them apart? Are there any gaps in the market that you can fill with your unique offerings? What is selling well now? What isn't moving at all? You'll need to understand how their offerings are performing so you'll have a better understanding of how to present and price yours.

Evaluate Profitability. While passion and skills are crucial, profitability is equally important. After all, your goal is to make money from your Etsy business. Research the average selling prices in your chosen niche and calculate your potential profit margins. At the time of this writing, Etsy charges 6.5% of the price you display for your item, plus any additional that you charge for shipping or gift wrapping. There are additional transaction fees, discussed later in the book. Whatever your cost of materials *and time* to create your items need to be low enough that you will recoup your investment, and make a profit. You want to aim for a 50 -100% mark-up to be profitable over time, depending on your category. Ensure that your chosen niche can sustain your financial goals.

Consider Market Trends. Etsy is ever evolving, with trends that come and go. Stay up to date with the latest market trends and see if you can incorporate them into your niche. We'll help you learn to research market trends. You're probably well aware of some already! Think about the calendar for the year. When are the gift giving occasions? When do people want to update their wardrobe? Trends are both topical, and time based. However, be cautious not to chase fleeting fads that might lead to short-lived success. If your product didn't exist a year ago, seriously consider if there will be significant demand a year from now. (Think Pet Rocks, Fidget Spinners, and other fast fads.)

Researching Trends And Customer Demand

Now that you've narrowed down your niche options, it's time to delve deeper into researching trends and customer demand. This step will help you fine-tune your niche and ensure that you're offering products that resonate with your target audience.

Explore Etsy's Trending Section. Etsy offers a handy "Trending" section that showcases the latest popular items. This is a goldmine of inspiration and insights into what customers are currently searching for. Keep an eye on this section to stay ahead of the curve. You may notice a theme (kitchen products), color (peach), or type of product (stickers) suddenly making a splash. You can adjust your items, headlines, or descriptions accordingly to make your items more likely to come up in trending searches.

Use Google Trends. Google Trends is a powerful free tool that can help you identify the seasonality and long-term interest in your niche. Google Trends allows you to analyze and track the popularity and interest of specific search terms or topics over time. It is not specific to Etsy. Instead, it shows trends across the internet. What is being searched, shopped for, and talked about? This research will help you use trending terms in your headlines and descriptions, so your items appear in more search results. You can compare the popularity of multiple search terms or topics to understand their relative interest levels. This is useful for competitive analysis. Google Trends categorizes search terms into various categories, making it easier to explore trends within specific industries or niches.

Check out a tool called erank. Register for a free account, and you'll be able to get a snapshot of the most popular products on Etsy. From there, upgrade your account ($5.99/mo for a basic plan, $9.99/mo for pro at the time of this writing), and dive deep into erank's data on the most popular search terms and keywords. This can help you discover products that fit into your niche that you may not have considered. And since tastes change regularly, you'll want to keep an eye on what is joining or falling off the list over the space of a few weeks, and months.

Conduct Additional Keyword Research. Effective SEO (Search Engine Optimization) skills are essential for Etsy success. The Etsy search bar is the search engine customers will use to find your products! Use keyword research tools to discover popular search terms related to your niche to drive customers to your listings. Incorporate these keywords into your product titles, descriptions, and tags to improve your visibility in Etsy's search results. There are over a dozen effective free tools out there. Use your favorite if you have one. If not, I recommend these free tools:

Google Keyword Planner: Google's Keyword Planner is a powerful tool for keyword research. While it's designed for Google Ads users, you can access it for free. It provides keyword suggestions, search volume data, and competition insights.

Ubersuggest: Ubersuggest is a user-friendly keyword research tool that offers keyword suggestions, search volume data, and competition metrics. It provides both basic and advanced keyword insights.

Keyword Surfer: Keyword Surfer is a Chrome browser extension that integrates with Google search. It displays keyword search volume and related keyword suggestions directly in your Google search results.

Analyze Customer Reviews. Don't underestimate the power of customer reviews. They offer a wealth of information! Analyze reviews of products similar to what you plan to sell. Pay attention to what customers praise and what they criticize. This feedback can guide you in refining your titles, descriptions, product offerings, and business model.

Leveraging Your Passions And Expertise

As I mentioned above, your niche should not only be profitable but also align with your passions and expertise. This alignment will keep you motivated and excited about your Etsy business, even during challenging times. It will make writing titles and item descriptions easier (you know the lingo in your discipline) and will help you in your interactions with your customers.

Create Unique and Authentic Products. Your passion and expertise can shine through in your creations. Customers are drawn to products that have a personal touch and are made with love and care. Infuse your personality and unique style into your items to set them apart.

Share Your Story. Part of the reason people shop on Etsy is to do business with crafters and makers directly. They want to know there is a real person behind the product. Share your journey, the inspiration behind your creations, and your expertise through your shop's "About" section. A compelling narrative can make customers feel more connected to your brand.

Continuous Learning and Improvement. Never stop learning and improving your craft. Take courses, attend workshops, and seek out resources to enhance your skills. This ongoing commitment to growth will not only benefit your products but also keep your passion alive. Likewise, Etsy is always evolving! Make sure to stay in line with product updates and news in the Seller Forums.

Stay True to Your Values. Don't be afraid to incorporate them into your business! Whether it's using sustainable materials or supporting a cause you're passionate about, aligning your business with your values can resonate with customers. Do you shop based on things made in the US, Christian based makers, or makers focused on sustainability? So do your customers!

Embrace Your Niche Journey. Remember, finding your niche is not a one-time task but an ongoing journey. Finding your niche on Etsy is an adventure that combines your passion, skills, and the potential for profit. It's the foundation upon which your successful Etsy business will be built. So, dive in with enthusiasm, do your research, and don't be afraid to adapt as you learn and grow. You may even do a little shopping on the way! Your creative journey on Etsy has just begun, and the possibilities are endless!

As you gain experience and insight into your chosen niche, you may discover new opportunities and directions for your Etsy business. Stay open to evolution and growth.

Perennially Popular Products On Etsy

Putting all of the above factors together, an image will start to emerge, like putting together a puzzle. What does it look like? All of these categories have been popular on Etsy since its founding. Are you considering jumping into one of these? They are competitive categories, so make sure your shop and your offerings stand out! Remember to be extremely specific in your keywords and descriptions to make sure you stand out from the crowd.

Handmade and personalized jewelry

Jewelry and craft supplies

Printables, Digital artwork, and Stickers

Notebooks and journals

Party decorations

Wedding products

Personalized cards and paper products

Personalized gifts

Handmade clothes

Handmade home décor

Fashion Accessories

Homemade bath and beauty products

Zero-waste and sustainable products

Vintage items

Baby and children's items

Digital Products

Selling digital products on Etsy has become an increasingly popular way for creative entrepreneurs to generate income. A digital product refers to any item that is delivered electronically rather than physically. These products are typically created and distributed in a digital format, such as downloadable files, and can include a wide range of items such as digital art prints, printable planners, digital patterns, e-books, digital photography, and more. When a customer purchases a digital product on Etsy, they receive access to download the file directly from the seller's shop or through a link provided by the seller. Digital products are a popular category on Etsy, offering buyers instant access to unique and customizable items without the need for physical shipping. Read on to learn whether you might want to offer digital products in your shop.

Why Digital Products Are Smart Inventory On Etsy

Low Overhead: Selling digital products requires minimal upfront investment compared to physical products. There are no manufacturing costs except your time to create the product, no shipping fees, and no inventory storage expenses. This makes it an attractive option for those looking to start a business on a budget.

Scalability: Once created, digital products can be sold an unlimited number of times without additional production costs. This scalability means that your earning potential can grow without a corresponding increase in workload.

Global Reach: Etsy's marketplace has a global customer base, allowing digital product sellers to reach a vast audience. This wide reach increases the chances of finding interested buyers for your digital products. If you're up for a global audience without international shipping, digital downloads make it easy!

Convenience: Buyers can download digital products immediately after purchase, providing instant gratification. This convenience factor often leads to higher sales, as customers do not have to wait for shipping.

Diverse Range of Products: Etsy caters to a diverse audience with various interests. Sellers can offer digital products in a wide range of niches, from art prints and digital planners to SVG files for crafters and downloadable templates for businesses.

What To Avoid When Choosing Your Niche

Choosing the perfect niche for your Etsy business is exciting, but it's equally important to know what to avoid, ensuring your journey is smooth and successful. This list will guide you through some potential pitfalls so you can make the best choices for your creative venture!

Consider Avoiding Overcrowded Niches. While it's tempting to jump into a niche that seems popular, be cautious about niches that are oversaturated with sellers. High competition can make it challenging to stand out and gain visibility. Instead, aim for a niche where you can offer a unique perspective or product that sets you apart from the crowd. Put a specific spin on your product, like "Children 0-3 yrs" or "Granny Chic" to drill down to a sub-niche where your buyers are looking.

Don't Neglect Market Research. One common mistake is diving headfirst into a niche without thorough research. Skipping this crucial step can lead to a mismatch between your products and what customers are looking for. Invest some time in researching your chosen niche on Etsy to understand customer demand and market trends. Search Google for articles about trends in your niche to help predict viability.

Don't Ignore Your Passion and Expertise. While it's wise to consider profitability, don't choose a niche solely for financial reasons if it doesn't align with your passions and expertise. If you're not genuinely interested in what you're selling, it can be challenging to stay motivated and creative over the long term. Remember, if you want to replace some or all of your current income, this could become your full time job. Make it something you love!

Avoid Overextending Yourself. Starting too broad and offering a wide range of products can overwhelm both you and your potential customers. Avoid the temptation to include everything under the sun in your shop. Start with a focused niche. Start with a very small range of products, and expand gradually as your business grows and you gain more experience.

Don't Forget About Target Audience. Your products should cater to a specific target audience, and your descriptions should speak to your audience directly. Avoid trying to appeal to everyone, as this can dilute your brand's identity and make marketing efforts less effective. Understand your ideal customer and tailor your products and marketing strategies to meet their needs and preferences.

Don't Rush the Decision. Choosing your niche is a significant decision, and it's essential not to rush it. Take your time to explore different options, research thoroughly, and reflect on what aligns best with your goals and passions. It's better to spend a little extra time upfront to make an informed decision than to regret it later. Your research and considerations may take days, weeks, or months depending on how much time you have for research.

Avoid Unrealistic Expectations. While I'm all about optimism, it's crucial to have realistic expectations when choosing your niche. First year sellers average about $1200 in sales due to the steep learning curve and the time it takes to create inventory. Building a profitable Etsy business takes time and effort. Don't expect overnight success or astronomical sales immediately, even when you've picked the perfect niche. Be patient, persistent, and prepared for both highs and lows. It takes time to build a following, collect reviews, and perfect your curated collection of products.

Don't Disregard Feedback and Data. Once your Etsy business is up and running, avoid the mistake of disregarding customer feedback and data. Listen to your customers' suggestions and reviews, and use the data provided by Etsy to make informed decisions about your products and shop improvements. It's the primary way you'll hear from your customers, and it's free advice!

In the exciting world of starting a profitable Etsy business, choosing the right niche is your foundation for success. By avoiding these common pitfalls, you'll set yourself up for a joyful and prosperous journey. Stay optimistic, stay creative, and remember that your niche should reflect your passions and expertise. With the right approach and a dash of enthusiasm, your Etsy venture is sure to thrive!

CHAPTER 2:
INVENTORY AND
CHOOSING YOUR
PRODUCT MIX

C ongratulations! Finding your niche was your first step. Now you need to populate your shop with items that will make sense for you as a seller in the long run. Ideally, you'll want a mix of active and passive income products. That is, you'll want a mixture of products that show your individual skill and creativity – and take time to produce, and some that once set up, make income for you with no additional effort at all.

How Much Inventory To Start With

When you open your Etsy shop, you need to consider the ideal amount of inventory to list. The right balance between the number of items, variety, and total dollar value of inventory can significantly impact your shop's visibility, customer engagement, and sales potential.

The number of items you should list in your Etsy shop depends on your capacity to create, source, and manage inventory. Starting with around 20 to 50 items is a good initial goal, depending on your price point and inventory mix. (Higher prices mean lower inventory will work, as sales will be at a slower pace.) This gives your shop a substantial presence and variety for customers to explore without overwhelming yourself. Gradually, you can increase the number of listings as you gain more experience and understand your market better.

Variety in your inventory is essential to cater to a broader customer base. Offering a mix of products within your niche or category can help attract different types of buyers. Consider listing variations of your products, such as different colors, sizes, or styles, to provide choices and meet various customer preferences. Consider natural combinations, like frames if you offer visual art. Bundle products together, like "Mom and Me" sewing patterns. This variety enhances the shopping experience and encourages repeat visits.

The total dollar value of your inventory should align with your budget and business goals. Don't overspend during start-up! You need to see what will sell! Instead, if you have limited inventory, wait to open your shop until you have created or curated more.

It's advisable to have a mix of both high and low-priced items. High-priced items can potentially bring in more revenue per sale, while lower-priced items can attract more customers and generate consistent sales. Ensure that your inventory investment remains sustainable, and you have the financial capacity to restock popular items.

Remember that quality trumps quantity. Focus on offering high-quality, unique, and well-presented products that resonate with your target audience. Continuously monitor your inventory's performance, adapt to market trends, and gather feedback from customers to refine your product offerings.

Good news! Many of the products sold on Etsy lend themselves to a mixed income stream of passive and active products. Read on to learn more about how you may want to manage your active and passive product inventory.

Active Income

Active income products in your Etsy shop refer to items that require ongoing effort, shipping, production, or customization on the seller's part for each sale. These products typically involve manual work or personalization, and the income generated is directly correlated with the time and effort invested. Active income products are the opposite of passive income products, which can be sold repeatedly with minimal ongoing effort once created. Here are some examples of active income products on Etsy:

Handmade Crafts: Products that are entirely crafted by the seller, such as hand-painted artwork, handmade jewelry, knitted scarves, or ceramic pottery, fall under active income products. Each item is created individually, and the seller must invest time and labor for each sale.

Customized Items: Products that require personalization or customization for each customer, such as engraved jewelry, monogrammed clothing, or custom-made wedding invitations, are considered active income products. Sellers need to tailor each item to the customer's specifications.

Made-to-Order or Bespoke Goods: Some sellers offer made-to-order or bespoke products, such as tailored clothing, custom furniture, or personalized home decor. These items are manufactured or customized based on individual customer requests, which makes them active income products.

Print-on-Demand Products: While print-on-demand services automate much of the production process, they still require active involvement. Sellers design their products, list them on

Etsy, and only produce items when customers place orders. Printing and shipping are outsourced to third-party companies.

Digital Customizations: Products like digital art commissions, custom graphic design work, or personalized digital templates (e.g., wedding invitations with customized names and dates) are active income products. Each customization is done on a per-order basis.

Photography Sessions or Original Photographs: If you offer photography services on Etsy, each session you book and carry out is an active income product. You must schedule and perform each shoot individually.

Consultation Services: If your Etsy shop offers services like wedding planning consultations, interior design advice, or personal styling sessions, these are considered active income products. They involve one-on-one time with clients.

Handmade Supplies: While some handmade supplies like beads or fabric can be considered passive income if they are sold in bulk, others like custom-made buttons or specialty fabric designs are active income products because they involve crafting or customization.

Art Commissions or Original Art: Selling original or commissioned artwork, where customers request specific paintings, illustrations, or sculptures, is an example of an active income product. Each commission or original piece is a unique project.

Vintage and Antique Items: While these are not actively produced, managing a shop that sells vintage or antique items can be considered active income because it involves sourcing, cleaning, photographing, and listing each item individually.

It's important to note that active income products require more time and attention from the seller than passive income products. However, *this is usually what you become known for!* Your personal creativity and artistic ability are what draws customers in. Sellers must factor in production time, customization, communication with customers, and order fulfillment when offering these products on Etsy. If these are the only products you will offer, your ability to produce or source products will be the controlling step in how much revenue you can generate. Active income products provide opportunities for creativity and a more personalized customer experience, which can be rewarding for both sellers and buyers. You will very likely want some ongoing production of active income products.

The drawback with physical products is that if you have a popular product, your shop may be empty periodically as you struggle to create enough inventory (called a stockout.) Additionally, you may not be able to physically produce enough product to make enough money to want to continue. That's where a blend of passive and active income products help. By combining both types of products, your shop will never be empty, and you'll be making money on your digital products for years after you create them.

Active Products With Passive Income Potential

Many physical products sold on Etsy can have related digital products for sale, creating an additional stream of passive income. The original piece or product will sell at a relatively high price, while the digital download will be less expensive, and likely, much more popular. Here are some examples of physical products on Etsy that can be complemented with related digital products:

Art Prints and Digital Art: If you create and sell physical art prints, you can also offer digital versions of your artwork for immediate download. Digital files can be offered in different resolutions for various purposes.

Printable Wall Art: This category includes digital art prints, posters, and illustrations that buyers can print at home or through a printing service. These can be sold alongside physical prints or as standalone items.

Journals and Planners: If you design and sell physical journals, planners, or notebooks, you can create digital versions of these planners that customers can print themselves. Digital planners can be customized, allowing users to fill in the details on their devices.

Stationery and Invitations: Physical stationery items such as greeting cards, wedding invitations, and thank-you cards can be complemented with digital templates. Buyers can customize these templates and print them at home or at a print shop.

Sewing Patterns: If you design and sell physical sewing patterns for clothing, accessories, or home decor items, you can create digital versions of these patterns. Digital patterns are convenient for customers who prefer immediate access and may be sold at a lower price point.

Crochet or Knitting Patterns: Similar to sewing patterns, crochet and knitting patterns for physical items can be turned into digital downloads. Crafters can have easy access to the instructions and reference them on their devices while working, or they can print them as needed.

Woodworking Plans: If you create and sell physical woodworking plans for furniture or decor items, consider offering digital versions. This allows woodworking enthusiasts to access the plans electronically and save on shipping costs.

Recipe Cards and Cookbooks: If you sell physical recipe cards or cookbooks, you can create digital versions that customers can access on their devices. Digital cookbooks may include interactive features like clickable links and search functions.

Printable Party Decorations: Sellers of physical party decorations can offer digital versions of their products, such as banners, invitations, and cupcake toppers. Customers can personalize these items and print them for their events.

Handmade Jewelry and Craft Supplies: While physical jewelry pieces and craft supplies are the primary products, you can create digital tutorials or guides on how to use and care for the products. This adds educational value to your offerings.

Woodworking Products: If you are a wood artist, your primary products may be puzzles, toys or tools. Your digital products may be patterns, designs, and how-to manuals.

Photography Prints and Digital Files: If you are a photographer selling physical prints, consider offering digital versions of your photos as well. Customers can purchase high-resolution digital files for personal or commercial use.

Physical Books and eBooks: If you are an author, you can sell physical copies of your books alongside digital eBook versions.

This provides readers with the option to choose their preferred format.

Clothing and Sewing Patterns: For clothing designers, selling both physical garments and the sewing patterns for those garments as digital downloads can be a successful strategy.

Handmade Crafts and DIY Kits: If you create handmade crafts like candles, soap, or embroidery kits, consider offering digital guides or tutorials that teach customers how to make similar items themselves. These recipes, how-to booklets, and webinars are very popular to bundle with kits, or sell on their own.

By offering related digital products alongside your physical items, you can cater to a broader audience, provide additional value to your customers, and create a diversified income stream on Etsy. Just ensure that your digital products are high-quality and add value to your customers' experience. Make sure they match your shop's theme and aesthetics, and you should make some sales!

Passive Income

Digital products are considered passive income. Passive income refers to earnings generated with minimal or no active involvement or ongoing effort on the part of the recipient. It is income that comes in regularly without requiring continuous work or active participation to maintain or increase it. Once you set it up, it continues to work for you, day in and day out. Here are some reasons digital products act as passive income on Etsy.

Front-Loaded Work: Most of the effort goes into creating the digital product initially. Once it's listed on Etsy, it can continue to sell without your constant involvement. Create a strong catalogue of products for your category, and then you can work as often or as little as you like. You just sit back and collect the income.

Automated Delivery: Etsy handles the delivery of digital products to customers. After purchase, buyers receive an automatic download link, eliminating the need for manual delivery.

No Physical Inventory: You don't have to worry about managing inventory, restocking, or dealing with damaged goods. Your inventory lives on your computer, and Etsy's. Digital products are infinitely replicable.

Time Flexibility: You can create and list digital products at your own pace, allowing you to balance your Etsy business with other commitments.

Digital products are created in a variety of programs from advanced imaging products like Photoshop to simple word processing programs. Consider your skillset, your passions, and your creativity, and you may have what it takes to create compelling digital products!

Themed Shops

As you consider the type of shop you want to run, you may want to offer a variety of things under a single heading. For example, if you run a wedding shop, you may want to include a mix of active and passive products for people getting married. These products cater to various aspects of wedding planning, décor, attire, and more. Here are some common physical products you can find in wedding shops on Etsy:

Wedding Invitations: Customizable wedding invitation suites, including save-the-date cards, RSVP cards, and thank-you notes, often featuring unique designs and personalized details. These can be physical or digital products.

Wedding Decor: Various decorative items such as table centerpieces, candles, garlands, banners, signage, and photo booth props that enhance the wedding venue's ambiance. These can also be physical, or printable from digital files.

Bridal Accessories: A wide array of bridal accessories, including veils, headpieces, tiaras, hairpins, garters, and jewelry sets to complete the bride's look. These could be handmade, vintage, or a blend.

Wedding Favors: Personalized wedding favors like mini bottles of wine, engraved keychains, custom candles, and unique trinkets for guests to take home as mementos. Personalized downloadable sticker designs are a digital option to go with your physical offerings.

Bridal Party Gifts: Gifts for bridesmaids, groomsmen, and other members of the wedding party, such as personalized robes, custom mugs, monogrammed tote bags, and jewelry.

Wedding Dresses and Attire: Custom-made wedding dresses, bridesmaid dresses, flower girl dresses, groomsmen suits, and accessories like bow ties and cummerbunds. Along with, or instead of, physical clothes, you can offer digital patterns and designs for all of the above.

Wedding Rings and Bands: Handcrafted wedding bands and engagement rings, often featuring unique designs, gemstones, and personalized engravings.

Wedding Stationery: Beyond invitations, this category includes seating charts, place cards, menu cards, and wedding programs, often coordinated with the overall wedding theme. Digital downloads of all of these are popular products, too.

Wedding Cake Toppers: Custom cake toppers featuring the bride and groom in various styles, such as figurines, silhouettes, or personalized wooden pieces.

Wedding Signs: Hand-painted or digitally designed signs for directing guests, displaying ceremony details, and adding personalized touches to the venue.

Guest Books and Alternative Guest Books: Traditional guest books as well as alternative options like fingerprint trees, wish cards, and photo guest books.

Wedding Ceremony Accessories: Products such as unity candles, sand ceremony sets, ring bearer pillows, and aisle runners for the wedding ceremony.

You get the idea. You can offer quite a bit of digital product along with your physical product to make your shop more popular with shoppers interested in all price points, or in doing some of the work themselves.

Headings That Host Profitable Digital Products

The profitability of digital products on Etsy depends on the niche. There are thousands, but some popular categories include:

Printables: Wall art, planners, calendars, journals, and educational resources.

Templates: Business card templates, resume templates, social media templates, stencil templates, spreadsheet and word processing templates, and website themes.

Digital Art: Illustrations, clipart, and digital brushes for artists and designers.

Crafting and Scrapbooking: SVG files, digital papers, and cut files for crafters.

EBooks: Self-published books, guides, and tutorials.

SVG Files: SVG files for cutting machines like Cricut and Silhouette for crafting and DIY projects.

Clipart and Illustrations: Graphic designers and artists often sell clipart, illustrations, and design elements for various creative projects.

Photography Presets: Digital presets for photo editing, particularly for Instagram aesthetics and Lightroom, are popular among both photographers and influencers.

Educational Resources: Digital educational materials, such as worksheets, lesson plans, and homeschooling resources.

Digital Art: Digital art downloads, including digital paintings, illustrations, and custom portraits, were a growing category on Etsy.

Digital Embroidery Designs: Downloadable digital artwork converted into a stitch pattern which can be used by embroidery machines to stitch incredibly detailed art on fabric.

Knitting, Crochet, and Sewing Patterns: Charts, designs, and instructions for sewing, knit, and crochet projects.

Woodworking and House Plans: Detailed plans and instructions for building and woodworking projects.

Planner and Productivity Pages: Worksheets for planners for weddings, graduations, business, schoolwork, and more.

Meal Planners and Recipe Cards: Meal planners to organize your diet and cooking plans, and create automated shopping lists. Recipe cards to fill in on your computer and print to share.

Remember that the popularity of specific digital products can vary by season and emerging trends.

I hope this has given you some ideas about how to consider populating your shop. I can't tell you exactly how you want to balance your physical and digital product mix, but I strongly recommend offering both. This allows you to have a little more flexibility in how many hours you work creating your physical products, because your income stream will be split between both digital and physical products.

CHAPTER 3: FACING THE COMPETITION

E tsy is a treasure trove of opportunities, but it's also a bustling marketplace with intense competition. Don't fret! In this chapter I'll walk you through the art of navigating competing shops and products on Etsy. By the end, you'll be equipped with the knowledge and strategies to set yourself apart and thrive on this platform.

Etsy hosts millions of sellers worldwide, all vying for the attention of shoppers. It's like a giant mall filled with talented vendors showcasing their wares. While competition can be intimidating, it's also a testament to the platform's vast potential for success.

Stand Out From Your Competition On Etsy

First and foremost, understand that competition is a part of any marketplace. It's a sign that there's demand for what you offer. Instead of viewing competitors as rivals, see them as peers who share the same passion for creativity.

Passion is your secret weapon on Etsy. When you love what you do, it shines through in your work, setting you apart from competitors. Create and curate products that make your heart sing, and your enthusiasm will resonate with customers. Use your passion in your product titles and descriptions, too. As a platform that people read and look at, instead of watching, choosing influential and exciting language and great images makes all the difference.

Tags/Keywords

As of this writing, on Etsy listings you have up to 13 keywords to use that help you get 'found' online. Getting this right is crucial! These keywords are very important because they draw attention to and describe your item in the search. You want to use these keywords in every title and description. Color, size, shape, and material are examples. There is a 20 character limit to each keyword, so single words or short 2-3 word phrases are good. (It doesn't have to be a single word!) You want to use words buyers will use when searching for something. Use simple words, not any industry jargon. Remember, many of your shoppers may be looking for a gift, and will be less familiar with "insider" language.

Titles

You might *want* to 'title' your work "The Warmth of the

Cosmos." That may speak to your soul or your creative process, but that isn't how people would search for a cozy blanket. Instead, your title needs to describe the product for sale. A better title in this example would be: Down Throw – Cozy Throw. That includes two variations in one title. Cozy Throw isn't specific, but it's popular. Down Throw is more specific. Having both can help. You can customize and personalize, but less is more.

Photos

Use clear, well-lit, and professional-quality photographs that showcase your products from various angles. Use plain backgrounds, and high resolution. A blurry cell phone snapshot will not sell product, and may make buyers question the quality of your products. High-quality images not only make your listings more appealing but also instill confidence in potential buyers. Check out the photos on the cover of this book. High contrast and high resolution can really make your work pop in an image!

Additionally, whenever possible, only use images of the exact product your buyer will receive. (In digital downloads there will be variations based on printer quality.) Buyers notice everything! If you have made 20 of an item and don't want to photograph them all, indicate in the description that it is a "representative" image.

Product Descriptions

Write comprehensive and accurate product descriptions that

include essential details such as size, color, materials, and care instructions. (Customers will leave negative reviews if they try to clean their product and the color comes off, it shrinks, or falls apart!) Highlight what makes your item unique, and its potential uses. Explain how it was made, or the specifics of its history. Help your customers think creatively about how to use your item, or who they might want to give it to as a gift. Great descriptions sell products. Flat descriptions tend to dampen enthusiasm. If you're unsure, ask a friend or loved one to read your description before you post, and give you some feedback. You'll get better with time!

Trends

Keep an eye on trending products and changing customer preferences. Be open to adapting your offerings to meet evolving demands. You never know when a particular product or niche is going to take off! Depending on your inventory levels and how long it takes you to create a new product, you may want to adapt seasonally, or more often. Use keywords that are 'trending,' even if that means you have to update your descriptions. Etsy has e-mail newsletters that highlight current trends - capitalize on this! (There are lots of Etsy topic newsletters outside of Etsy, too. Many are helpful to Etsy shop owners. Google 'em and sign up!)

Stay up to date with Etsy's Seller Handbook and forums for valuable insights. And follow Google Trends to know what's trending over the last 30, 60, or 90 days.

Quality

Remember, it's not about flooding your shop with products, but instead it's about offering high-quality items that customers cherish. Quality products can fetch higher prices and generate repeat business. They also generate the best reviews. And when you're shopping, don't you look at reviews? So will your buyers!

Aesthetic and Branding

Craft a memorable brand story, logo, and shop aesthetics that reflect your unique style. Your brand identity can make a lasting impression and attract loyal customers. All these elements combine to create a mood and atmosphere for your shop. There are several online logo design tools that offer free services for creating logos. Some popular options include *Canva, Looka* (formerly *Logojoy*), *Hatchful* by Shopify, and *Designhill Logo Maker*. Choose one that suits your preferences and experience level.

Make sure to open accounts on social media in your shop's name, and post often! Use your logo and shop description everywhere to expand your brand recognition. (More on this in Chapter 5: Mastering Marketing.)

Frequent Listing Updates: Keep your shop fresh by regularly adding new listings and updating existing ones. Etsy tends to favor active and frequently updated shops in search rankings. This means if you update your inventory and descriptions, Etsy will score your listings higher, and post them closer to the top of the results. This substantially increases your chances of being seen! You need to get found first, before your item can be chosen.

Keep your listings up to date!

Blog

Consider creating a blog to support your Etsy shop. Each post doesn't have to be long, but the blog should be branded with your shop name and logo, and you'll have to create short content. Post consistently, at least once per week. Tell the story of what, how, and why you do what you do. Use photos! Your customers want to know you. A growing percentage of the most successful shops on Etsy have their own blogs, and many have massive followings. You can share how-to tips, creative inspirations, and insight into upcoming products. It will take time to gain traction (often 6 months to a year) but don't lose heart. You're in this for the long haul, right?

Analyze Your Competitors

Now that you've worked to differentiate yourself from the competition, let's delve into the art of analyzing your competitors. Understanding your peers can help you identify opportunities and make informed decisions.

Start by identifying the top sellers in your niche or category. Explore their shops, read their reviews, and take note of what sets them apart. Look for common trends and unique selling points. Do they tell a great story? Do they have more pictures than others? Do they describe their products using sensory words about smell, sound, or feel? The top sellers in your niche probably have some key points in common. Make notes, and learn from their success.

Study your competitors' pricing strategies. Are they offering premium products at higher prices, or are they focusing on affordability? Understanding pricing dynamics in your niche can help you position your products effectively. You may want to come in at the highest quality and price point, or you may want to be an economical option. Understanding their pricing helps you position yourself to attract your target buyers.

Customer reviews are a goldmine of information. Analyze what customers love about your competitors' products and any areas where they might fall short. Use this feedback to fine-tune your offerings. This is ongoing homework! This is another place where you'll learn how your market may be changing, and exactly what they're looking for next.

Evaluate the shipping options and delivery times of your competitors. Can you offer faster shipping or unique packaging that sets you apart? Great customer experience can give you a competitive edge. People care about packaging! Knowing their product will arrive in good shape is key to buyer confidence. Think about it – if a review mentions that an item arrived broken, wouldn't you have second thoughts about placing an order?

Examine your competitors' marketing strategies. Are they active on social media, running promotions, or participating in Etsy sales events? This is going to take a little more research, but a Google search is a great place to start. Learning from their marketing tactics and applying them yourself can help you reach a broader audience.

All of this research is to help you learn who is on top, and how they got there. It's different in every niche! The more you learn about your direct competitors, the better you can showcase your strengths to your customers/

Showcase Your Unique Style

Embrace your individuality and let your creativity shine. Develop a signature style that distinguishes your products from the rest. Your distinct aesthetic will attract customers who resonate with your vision. There are many ways to unify your products into a single aesthetic. Read on to create your signature style.

Consider offering customization or personalization options for your products. Personalization is popular in many niches, like children's apparel and décor. It's also a major driver in gift giving. Personalized items add a personal touch that sets you apart and often commands higher prices.

Introduce limited-edition or one-of-a-kind items to your shop. Limited availability can create a sense of urgency among buyers and drive sales. If your offering is collectible or artistic, limited editions will command higher prices.

Share your story and the inspiration behind your creations in their description, or in your shop's About section. Customers love connecting with artisans on a personal level, and your story can forge that connection. Consider including the product story or brand story on a decorative card insert when shipping your products. Your shoppers will be both end users and people giving the item as a gift, so the cards can help the recipient of gifts shop with you in the future. I have received business from gift recipients in every one of my shops, and they often become steady customers!

Providing exceptional customer service is a surefire way to stand out. Respond to inquiries promptly. This means less than 24 hours, and under 12 is best. Resolve issues gracefully. There will be customers who misread the listing, misunderstand the terms, or change their mind about something. You need to make them feel heard and respected. Go the extra mile to make customers feel valued! It will show in your reviews.

Consider bundling complementary products together. This can encourage customers to purchase more items from your shop and increase your average order value, as well as decrease your shipping costs. It's also thoughtful of you to anticipate your customer's needs. If others in your space aren't offering bundles, all the better!

Marketing

There's a whole chapter on marketing in this book – Chapter 5. It's the last step in remaining competitive. We'll get there in a few minutes! All of what we've discussed here are ways to stand out in the Etsy listings without spending money on promotion, or time on marketing. This is where you need to begin. All the marketing and promotion you do relies on you managing these basics effectively.

In your journey as an Etsy seller, embrace healthy competition, stay true to your passion, and adapt to changing trends. Analyze your competitors to gain insights and fine-tune your strategies. Most importantly, set yourself apart with a unique style, personalized offerings, and exceptional customer service.

As you continue your creative endeavors on Etsy, keep in mind that success takes time and persistence. Stay positive! You can do this!

CHAPTER 4: PRICING STRATEGY

I t's no surprise that pricing is a critical aspect of running a successful Etsy shop, especially for new shop owners. Understanding pricing makes the difference between thinking a product has long term viability, and knowing it does. It's essential to find a balance between setting prices that attract buyers and ensuring that your shop remains profitable. In this analysis, I'll discuss various aspects of pricing strategies for a new Etsy shop owner. You'll need to account for your total costs to produce each product, and your business expenses and taxes.

Registering Your Business

First off, you'll need to register your business. These are the first start-up costs to consider in your pricing strategy.

Registering a business in the United States involves several steps and considerations, including choosing a legal structure, obtaining necessary licenses and permits, and registering a DBA (Doing Business As) if applicable. None of the steps are difficult, and requirements vary by state. Here is an overview of the process along with approximate costs:

Choose a Business Structure: The first step is to decide on the legal structure for your business. Common options for an Etsy business include:

- Sole Proprietorship
- Partnership
- Limited Liability Company (LLC)

Each structure has its advantages and disadvantages in terms of liability, taxation, and management. Consult with a legal or financial advisor to determine the best fit for your business.

Register Your Business Name: If you plan to operate under a name different from your legal name (e.g., "John Smith" doing business as "Smith's Wood Creations"), you may need to register a DBA or a fictitious business name. The process and cost for this can vary by state and locality but typically range from $10 to $100. This affords you some anonymity with your customers, and protects your privacy.

Obtain an EIN (Employer Identification Number): An EIN, also known as a Federal Tax Identification Number, is required for most business structures. It's used for tax purposes, opening a business bank account, and hiring employees. You can obtain an EIN for free from the IRS. Just fill out the paperwork.

Register with State Authorities: Depending on your state, you may need to register your business with the appropriate state agency. This may involve paying a state filing fee, which varies by state but is typically between $50 and $300.

Get Necessary Licenses: The permits and licenses required can vary widely depending on your location. Commonly you may require a business license. Costs can range from $50 to approximately $200 as of this writing, depending on your location.

Register for State and Local Taxes: You may need to register for state sales tax, payroll tax, or other applicable taxes. These registrations are typically free, but you'll need to comply with ongoing tax requirements.

Open a Business Bank Account: To separate your personal and business finances, it's a good idea to open a business bank account. Some banks may charge monthly fees, while others offer free business checking accounts.

Comply with Ongoing Requirements: After initial registration, your business will have ongoing compliance requirements, including annual reports, taxes, and renewing licenses and permits. They sound intimidating, but are usually one page or less for Etsy businesses. Be sure to stay informed about these obligations to avoid penalties or legal issues.

Costs and Fees: The costs associated with registering a business can vary widely based on factors like location, legal structure, and industry. On average, you might expect to spend anywhere from $100 to $300 or more in total, including registration fees, permits, and legal assistance.

Keep in mind that these steps and costs are approximate and can vary depending on your specific circumstances and location. It's essential to research and understand the requirements in your area and consider seeking professional advice to ensure you comply with all necessary regulations and start your business on the right foot.

Choose A Pricing Strategy

There are any number of pricing strategies out in the Etsy community, but I'd like to focus on the 3 parts of standard pricing structures. They are cost based pricing, competitive pricing and analysis, and value based pricing. You'll want to consider, and perhaps incorporate all of them in your initial pricing plan.

Cost-Based Pricing

Start by calculating your costs, including material, labor (you need to pay yourself a living wage), overhead, and Etsy fees. This forms the foundation of your pricing. The standard markup over cost varies by industry and product type, but a common rule of thumb is a 50% markup, meaning you'd set your selling price at 1.5 times your total costs. In many retail disciplines, the standard is 100%. However, this may need to be adjusted depending on your niche, competition, and perceived value of your products.

Here's what you need to consider in your cost-based pricing:

Material Costs: Calculate the cost of materials used for each product. This includes maintaining, depreciating, or purchasing the tools you need for your work. Keep track of variations in material prices, especially if they fluctuate due to market conditions. This will affect your pricing, which you will want to keep constant. Any shipping costs to get your tools and materials to you should also be included.

Labor Costs: Estimate the time it takes to make each product and assign an hourly wage to your labor. This can be challenging for creative work, but it's crucial to ensure you're not underpricing your time and skills. It's critical to pay yourself a living wage in these calculations!

Overhead Costs: Include expenses like shipping supplies, any additional equipment maintenance, and marketing costs in your pricing calculations. If you work in a studio, your rental costs and transportation should be included. Spread these costs across your products to ensure they're covered.

Shipping Costs: Consider shipping expenses when setting your prices. Decide whether you'll offer free shipping and include it in the product price, or charge shipping separately. Shipping will vary widely across the country and around the world. If your product is over 2 lbs., consider charging separately for shipping.

Etsy Fees:

Listing Fee: Etsy charges a small fee for listing each item in your shop. These fees can add up, especially if you have a large inventory. Listings typically last for four months or until the item is sold. When an item is relisted, the fee is charged again. At the time of this writing, the fee per item is $0.20.

Transaction Fee: Etsy charges a transaction fee on each sale, which includes a percentage of the item's sale price (including shipping and gift wrapping costs). The transaction fee varies by location and currency but is usually around 6.5% as of 2024.

Payment Processing Fee: If you use Etsy Payments, Etsy charges a payment processing fee for processing the payment from the buyer. This fee covers credit card processing and varies by location but is typically around 3% plus $0.25 per sale.

Currency Conversion Fees: If you sell internationally and deal with different currencies (like selling to Canada or Mexico,) you may incur additional fees for currency conversion when you withdraw funds.

Shipping label fees: In the US and some other countries you have the option of purchasing Etsy branded shipping labels through Etsy. Fees apply, and vary based on nation, and whether you choose a private shipper, like FedEx, or the national mail.

Etsy Plus or Premium Features: Etsy offers subscription plans, such as Etsy Plus and Etsy Premium, which come with additional features and tools. These plans have monthly fees that should be accounted for.

Taxes: Etsy income is taxable, so you should set aside a portion of your earnings to cover income taxes. The specific tax rate depends on your location and income level, but if you're in the 17% tax bracket, set aside 17% of your gross until you become accustomed to what deductions you can take.

Advertising Costs: If you run paid advertising campaigns to promote your Etsy shop or individual listings, you'll need to budget for advertising expenses.

Photography and Graphics: High-quality product photos and branding materials may require investments in professional photography equipment or graphic design services.

Refund Processing: If you offer refunds or returns, consider the associated costs, including return shipping and refund processing fees assessed by Etsy.

Office Supplies: Expenses like printer ink, paper, and office supplies may be necessary for managing your Etsy shop. If you use specialized equipment or software, maintenance costs should be considered.

It's essential to keep meticulous records of all your expenses for tax and planning purposes. Regularly review your shop's financial performance to ensure that you're pricing your products effectively and maintaining a profitable Etsy shop. Properly accounting for these overlooked costs will help you make informed business decisions and achieve long-term success.

Competitive Pricing and Analysis

In addition to understanding all of your costs as listed above, research competitors in your niche to understand their pricing strategies. Look at both established shops and new entrants. Identify the average price range for similar products, and use this information to inform your pricing decisions. You can choose to price slightly below, within, or slightly above the average, depending on your unique selling points.

Value-Based Pricing

In addition to understanding all of your costs as listed above, consider the unique value your products offer to customers. Are they handmade, customizable, or of exceptionally high quality? If so, you may be able to charge a premium price compared to alternatives. Emphasize these unique selling points in your product descriptions to justify higher prices. Plenty of people want premium products, but they must understand what makes them premium to agree to pay more.

Now that you've considered pricing, you can assess the value of keeping different items in your shop. Recognizing that your mark up over cost will probably be somewhere between 50 and 100%, some items may seem more attractive than others. Small items with low profit may take as long to package and ship as large ones, meaning they have a higher overhead cost to process by percentage.

1 small item priced at $5 may take 10 minutes to package, label, and ship. Another item, priced at $30 also takes 10 minutes. If you pay yourself $30 per hour, it took $5.00 of your time to process either item! You'll need to do some careful math on each item to reveal its potential profitability.

Sales, Discounts, And Promotions

Offering discounts, sales, and coupons can be powerful strategies to attract customers, increase sales, and promote your Etsy shop. You'll want to use these strategies thoughtfully, considering your objectives, profitability, and customer preferences, to ensure they contribute positively to your shop's growth and success.

Like everything in business, there are some key considerations when planning some sort of pricing discount.

Profit Margin: Always calculate the impact of discounts, sales, or coupons on your profit margin. Ensure that your discounted prices are still profitable, even after applying the discount. Consider your cost of goods, overhead, and desired profit margin when setting sale prices.

Customer Segmentation: Consider creating targeted discounts or coupons to attract a particular target audience, or for different customer segments, such as new customers, loyal customers, or high-value customers.

Timing and Frequency: Avoid excessive discounting, as it can devalue your products and erode your brand's perceived value. Use discounts strategically and monitor their frequency. Strategically time your discounts and sales. Common opportunities include seasonal sales (e.g., holiday or back-to-school), clearance events, and anniversary sales for your shop.

Measuring Success: Track the performance of your discounts and coupons. Analyze sales data to determine their impact on revenue, customer acquisition, and customer retention.

Terms and Conditions: Clearly communicate the terms and conditions of your discounts and coupons to customers to avoid misunderstandings or disputes.

Promotion: Your great deals won't sell well if no one knows about them! Promote your sale through various channels, including your Etsy shop's announcement section, social media, email marketing, and paid advertising if it aligns with your budget.

Urgency and Scarcity: Create a sense of urgency by specifying a limited time for the sale or emphasizing limited stock. This can motivate buyers to make a purchase quickly.

Transparent Pricing: Be transparent with customers about the original and discounted prices. Etsy allows you to show the previous price alongside the discounted one, which can help build trust.

Sales

Offer discounts during holidays, special occasions, or relevant seasons to attract more buyers. Consider themed promotions or bundles to increase sales. Sale prices should be placed on items you want to draw attention to, and/or want to sell more of. This will decrease your profit margin, so be thoughtful about how much of your stock you put on sale at any time.

Determine the purpose of your discount or sale. It could be to clear out old inventory, boost sales during a slow period, attract new customers, or reward loyal ones.

Consider different types of discounts:

Percentage Off: Offer a percentage discount on selected items or the entire shop.

Fixed Amount Off: Provide a specific dollar amount discount.

Buy One, Get One (BOGO): Encourage customers to purchase more by offering a free or discounted item with a qualifying purchase.

Coupon Codes

Create coupon codes for repeat customers or as a reward for social media followers. This can incentivize customer loyalty. These are usually for a small percentage, or a limited time to encourage urgency to return to your shop.

Coupon Types: Etsy provides several types of coupons, including:

Percentage Off: This type offers a percentage discount on the total purchase.

Fixed Amount Off: Provides a specific dollar amount discount.

Free Shipping: Offers free shipping on qualifying orders.

Targeting: You can create coupons for specific customers, use them in marketing campaigns, or share them with repeat buyers to encourage return purchases.

Minimum Purchase: Set a minimum purchase amount for the

coupon to be applied. This can help boost your average order value.

Coupon Codes: Choose unique and easy-to-remember coupon codes, as they can be an essential part of your marketing strategy. Consider "MomLove" for Mother's Day, as an example.

Expiration Dates: Specify clear expiration dates for your coupons. This can create a sense of urgency and encourage customers to use them promptly.

Combine with Sales: You can combine coupons with ongoing sales for extra savings, which can be an enticing offer for customers.

Bundle Deals

Bundle related products together and offer them at a slightly lower price than if purchased individually. This can encourage customers to buy more, save on shipping costs, and increase value for the customer.

Limited-Time Offers

Create a sense of urgency with flash sales or limited-time discounts. Be sure to communicate the expiration date clearly to encourage quick purchases.

Pricing strategies for an Etsy shop should be dynamic (ongoing and changing.) Every change should be well-researched process. Balancing competitive pricing, covering costs, and offering attractive promotions can help your new shop attract customers, make a profit, and establish a strong presence on the platform. Remember to continuously monitor your pricing strategies and adjust them as your business grows and evolves.

CHAPTER 5:
MASTERING
MARKETING YOUR
ETSY SHOP

Whether you're a seasoned Etsy seller or just starting, effective marketing is the key to unlocking the full potential of your shop. In this chapter, I'll walk you through strategies to market your Etsy shop and products. Let's dive in and take your creative venture to new heights.

Why Marketing In Year One Is Tough

You may not want to do much paid marketing in year 1, but that doesn't mean you won't be marketing! In your first year, you'll be working to build your shop, your inventory, and your organic following. It takes some time to work the kinks out, and really feel like you know what you're doing.

Getting your shop noticed by potential customers can take time and effort. It's not uncommon for new shops to experience long periods of slow sales, especially in the beginning. Patience is key during these times, and cash flow from the business is usually inconsistent.

Learning to effectively use SEO (search engine optimization) to improve your shop's visibility within Etsy and on social media can be a steep learning curve depending on the complexity of your niche. This can take months to do well. Different keyword combinations will have to be tried, and given a chance to work (6 weeks) to be sure you're using the most successful ones. It may click at the beginning, or it make take quite a while.

Balancing inventory and managing supplies can be tricky, especially if you have fluctuating demand for your products. And then there are the questions of where do you store it all, photograph it all, and write your product listings, and posts about it? It takes a little time and practice to get the balance right.

Determining the right pricing strategy to cover your costs and make a profit while remaining competitive can be challenging. It may take time to find the sweet spot. Some businesses do well from the beginning, but others struggle to be competitive.

Running an Etsy shop requires time for product creation, order fulfillment, customer communication, and marketing.

Balancing these tasks, especially if you have other commitments, can be demanding.

With all of this going on, you may not want to lean into the paid marketing side too hard at the beginning. Be kind to yourself, and accept that there is a lot to learn! Start with the free and very low cost marketing of optimizing your shop.

Optimize Your Shop

Start by optimizing your Etsy shop itself. All the promotion in the world will not help you if your titles and listings are poor.

Use relevant keywords in your shop title, product titles, listings, and tags to improve your shop's visibility in Etsy's search results. Choose an eye-catching and memorable shop banner and profile picture that reflect your brand. Ensure your shop policies, shipping information, and return policies are clear and customer friendly.

Invest time in capturing stunning, well-lit product photos. If your photos are of poor quality, you will have a hard time finding buyers. Use multiple angles to showcase your items and ensure they look their best. If you aren't a good photographer, talk to a friend or relative. See if they can help you improve, or take photos for you. Learn more about photography by reading photography blogs, and in the "Photographing Your Items" chapter in this book.

Seek inspiration. Don't reinvent the wheel! Explore successful Etsy shops in your niche. Take note of their marketing strategies, branding, and product listings. How do they name their items? What kind of photos do they feature? Don't copy them, or do! Let their success inspire your approach.

Stay open to learning. Join Etsy Teams, which are groups of sellers with similar interests or niches. Read blogs, and attend webinars to gain insights into effective marketing techniques. Marketing is constantly evolving, and different outlets may be more effective in your niche. Some Etsy shops do well with Facebook posts, while others rely on Promoted Listings. Be willing to adapt and evolve your strategies.

Craft compelling and informative product descriptions that highlight the unique features and benefits of your items. Be sure to include relevant details like size, materials, and care instructions.

Encourage satisfied customers to leave reviews. You can do this in your shipping communications. A quick, "Thanks in advance for leaving an honest review!" will remind your buyers to leave feedback. Positive reviews build trust and credibility in your shop.

Build an email list of customers and interested buyers. This list is gold! These people have proven they are interested in spending money with you. They represent your most likely future buyers. Offer incentives like discounts or freebies in exchange for email subscriptions. Send out regular newsletters with product updates, promotions, and exclusive offers to keep your audience engaged and informed.

Etsy offers paid advertising options, such as Promoted Listings and Google Shopping Ads, which can increase your shop's visibility to potential buyers. Setting affordable budgets is easy! Experiment with these tools to find the most effective keywords and budget allocation. They are easy to use, and can be very effective at driving traffic when you are first starting out, as well as keeping traffic flowing once your shop is established.

The Power Of Social Media

Social media can be your ticket to connecting with a vast and eager audience. Platforms like Pinterest, TikTok, Facebook, and Instagram can amplify your message organically, through posts, and through paid advertising campaigns. You'll want to establish a presence on the channels your target audiences frequent. (This is just an overview. For a more detailed explanation, I love *Social Media Marketing for Dummies,* by Shiv Singh and Stephanie Diamond.)

Choose the right platforms. Identify which social media platforms align with your target audience and product niche. (Not sure which platforms are best for your audience? Ask Google, or ChatGPT.) For visual crafts, Instagram and Pinterest are fantastic choices. If you sell digital products, Twitter and Facebook might work well. Some target audiences are obsessed with TikTok. Wherever your market lives, create an account under your shop name, import contact and set your profile to "open" or "public" and get posting!

Once you have an account on a social media platform, find groups associated with your target market and your product offering. These groups are great resources to build up contacts and place posts about your shop and products.

Showcase your products in a visually appealing and authentic way. Use great photography, and be yourself. Share behind-the-scenes glimpses of your creative process to build a personal connection with your audience. People love to feel like an insider, and it's a great way to showcase quality and customization.

Regularly post content to keep your followers engaged. Use a content calendar to plan your posts and maintain a consistent brand presence. (That's a document that you create to remind you what content you want to post, and when, like mentioning an upcoming sale.) Most brands need to add content at least twice a week to maintain an audience, but some need to post more often. Let your audience engagement be your guide.

Respond to comments, messages, and questions promptly. Within the hour is best, and within 12 hours is the outside of good. Engaging with your audience helps build trust and loyalty. Keep your tone friendly and supportive, and remember to thank your audience for reaching out.

Research and use relevant hashtags to increase the discoverability of your posts. These are likely the same hashtags that are most effective on Etsy. (Use the tools mentioned in Chapter 1.) Don't forget to create a unique hashtag for your brand to encourage user-generated content, like pictures of your products in their homes! And invite people to follow or subscribe to your posts on platforms that allow it.

Paid Advertising On Social Media

Advertising your Etsy shop on Pinterest, Instagram, and Facebook, among others, can be a great way to increase visibility and drive traffic to your shop. These ads are generally low-cost, and may make sense during certain seasons, and for certain shops that need high volume to be profitable. Here's a step-by-step guide on how to advertise your Etsy shop on these social media platforms, along with some rationale for each:

1. Pinterest:

Pinterest is a visual platform where users actively search for inspiration and ideas. It's an excellent platform for showcasing your products and driving traffic to your Etsy shop, as users often click through to learn more about the products they discover.

Step-by-Step Actions:

a. Create a Pinterest Business Account: - If you don't already have one, create a Pinterest business account for your Etsy shop. This will give you access to Pinterest's advertising tools.

b. Pin High-Quality Images: - Pin images of your Etsy products with compelling visuals. Use high-resolution photos and create visually appealing Pins.

c. Optimize Pin Descriptions: - Write engaging and keyword-rich descriptions for your Pins. Include relevant hashtags and keywords related to your products, just like you do on Etsy.

d. Use Rich Pins: - Enable "rich pins" for your Etsy products, which provide additional information about your products, such as prices and availability.

e. Create Promoted Pins: - Set up and run Promoted Pins

campaigns to reach a wider audience. You can target specific demographics, interests, and keywords. It makes it easy to connect with your target audience.

f. Analyze and Adjust: - Use Pinterest Analytics to track the performance of your Pins and campaigns. Adjust your strategy based on the data to improve results.

2. Instagram:

Instagram is a highly visual platform with a massive user base, making it an ideal platform to showcase your products and engage with potential customers. In addition to static images, you can take advantage of "Reels" to show some ways to use your products, or some behind the scenes action.

Step-by-Step Actions:

a. Set Up an Instagram Business Account: - If you haven't already, convert your Instagram account into a business account. This gives you access to Instagram's advertising features and insights.

b. Create Visually Appealing Content: - Share high-quality images and videos of your Etsy products. Use Instagram Stories, Reels, and regular posts to diversify your content. Video gets higher engagement than images, so mix it up!

c. Use Relevant Hashtags: - Include relevant and trending hashtags in your captions to increase discoverability, just like you do on Etsy.

d. Engage with Your Audience: - Respond to comments,

messages, and engage with your followers to build a community around your brand. It makes a huge difference in the loyalty of your followers!

e. Run Instagram Ads: - Create and run Instagram ads using Facebook Ads Manager, which allows you to target specific demographics and interests. Reaching your target audience is as easy as filling in a form.

f. Measure Performance: - Use Instagram Insights to track the performance of your posts and ads. Adjust your content and strategy based on insights.

3. Facebook (Meta):

Facebook (Meta) has a vast user base and offers a wide variety of established groups in every imaginable niche. It offers robust advertising options, making it suitable for reaching a broad audience and retargeting potential customers.

Step-by-Step Actions:

a. Create a Facebook Page: - Set up a Facebook Page for your Etsy shop. Ensure it's complete with your shop's information, logo, and cover image.

b. Share Shop Updates: - Regularly post updates, product launches, and other engaging content on your Facebook Page to keep your audience informed.

c. Use Facebook Ads Manager: - Create and manage Facebook ad campaigns using Facebook Ads Manager. You can target specific demographics, interests, and behaviors. Like the above platforms, it's easy to describe and reach your target audience.

d. Run Retargeting Campaigns: - Use Facebook Pixel to track website visitors and create retargeting ads to re-engage users who visited your Etsy shop but didn't make a purchase.

e. Analyze Performance: - Monitor the performance of your Facebook ads using Ads Manager and Facebook Insights. Adjust your ad strategy based on data.

Remember to tailor your content and advertising strategy to each platform's unique audience and features. Consistency and engagement are key to building a strong online presence and driving traffic to your Etsy shop through these social media platforms.

Scaling Up Your Marketing Efforts

When you're first learning the ropes, you may be reluctant to spend time and/or money on marketing and advertising. That's perfectly normal. Go at your own pace. But at some point, you're probably going to want to make a clear plan to consistently drive buyers to your shop. Below are some ways to create your plan.

Define specific, measurable goals for your Etsy shop, such as increasing sales by 15%, expanding your customer base, or launching new product lines. You can make them as specific and time bound as you want. The more specific you make them, the clearer your path to success will be.

Accept that you may have to spend money. Be honest with yourself about what you can realistically afford, and how often you are willing to spend it. Make a budget.

Etsy offers paid advertising options like Promoted Listings and Google Shopping Ads. Additionally, a combined approach with social media advertising can be very effective. Work with Pay Per Click models to maximize exposure and limit costs. Experiment with these tools to increase your shop's visibility to potential buyers.

What To Put In Your Ads

Creating effective ads to drive traffic to your Etsy shop requires a thoughtful approach that captures the attention of your target audience and encourages them to take action. If you're not sure how to write a great ad, look at your competitors. Or, ask ChatGPT (free) to write you a few ads. Just tell it what you need it to do. A good prompt might look like this:

Write a 50 word ad for my handmade, vintage-style, wooden car children's toys. The price point is $28. Describe how the toy encourages imagination.

ChatGPT came back with this:

"Discover endless adventures with our handmade vintage-style wooden car toys! Crafted with care and nostalgia, these charming toys spark creativity in young minds. At just $28, they're the perfect gift to fuel imagination and take little ones on exciting journeys. Unleash the joy of play today!"

Add your image, and a "Click Here to Learn More" button, and you're done!

Below I explain several elements that can be combined to build a great ad. You don't need to put all of them in every ad! Numbers 1-4 are constant. The rest are things you can vary with your specific situation. Here's how to construct a good ad:

Compelling Imagery/Visuals

Use eye-catching visuals that showcase your products. High-quality images or videos that highlight your product's features, details, and how they're used can grab viewers' attention. You may want to use images of your product in use, or a particularly nice photo from your product listing. What is important is that it grabs attention in the context of the social media scrolling your customer is doing.

Clear Call-to-Action (CTA)

Include a clear and concise CTA that tells viewers what action you want them to take. Common CTAs for Etsy shop ads include "Shop Now," "Browse Our Collection," "Discover More," or "Shop the Sale." Ads without calls to action have a tiny fraction of the clicks of clear CTAs. Don't forget your CTA!

Link to Your Etsy Shop

Ensure that your ad includes a clickable link directly to your Etsy shop or a specific product listing. Whenever possible, make the image clickable, too. Make it easy for viewers to access your shop. A great CTA won't help if there's nothing to click!

Engaging Ad Copy

Write concise and engaging ad copy that complements your visuals. Address your target audience's pain points or desires and convey how your products can meet their needs. Use words that are sensory in nature, discussing how something feels, tastes, or smells. It engages the reader at a higher level.

Value Proposition

Highlight the unique value of your products. Explain what makes them special, such as their quality, craftsmanship, or unique features.

Limited-Time Offers and Promotions

If you have ongoing sales, discounts, or special promotions in your Etsy shop, make sure to mention them in your ads. Creating a sense of urgency can encourage clicks, and everyone loves a discount!

Relevant Hashtags

Use relevant and trending hashtags to increase the discoverability of your ad. Research popular hashtags in your niche and incorporate them into your ad copy.

Social Proof

If you have positive reviews or testimonials from customers, consider incorporating them into your ad. Social proof can build trust and credibility. It's easier to believe you if the reader doesn't need to take your word for it!

Branding Element

Your shop's logo or branding elements to reinforce brand recognition. Consistent branding helps viewers remember your shop.

Ad Format Selection:

Choose the appropriate ad format for your goals and platform. For example, on Instagram, you can use carousel ads to showcase multiple products or stories ads for a more immersive experience.

Targeted Audience:

Use social media advertising tools to target your ads to a specific audience. Define demographics, interests, behaviors, and other relevant factors to reach potential customers who are more likely to be interested in your products.

Tracking and Analytics:

Set up tracking for your ads to measure their performance. Platforms like Facebook Ads Manager and Google Analytics can provide valuable insights into click-through rates, conversions, and ROI. You'll be able to track which ads drove traffic, and which were not effective.

Controlling Costs Of Marketing

Effective marketing doesn't have to break the bank. Like all marketing, low cost marketing takes time. If you're not in a hurry, you can build a lot of organic traffic using the methods above. Here are some more ideas.

As I mentioned above, you may not want to spend much time or money in the first year while you work the kinks out of running your business. After your first year, allocate a portion of your earnings specifically for marketing. Having a predefined budget ensures you're not overspending. (In your first year, you'll be working to build your shop, your inventory, and your organic following.)

DIY. Many marketing tasks can be handled in-house without hiring expensive professionals. Learn to create your own marketing materials and run your campaigns. If you're really stuck, consider hiring a marketing student from an area college through a website like Fiverr.

Keep a close eye on the return on investment (ROI) for your marketing efforts. Focus on strategies that generate the most revenue while minimizing costs.

Craft engaging and shareable social media content, including high-quality images, videos, and blog posts related to your products. Share your creative process and behind-the-scenes stories to connect with your audience.

Build an email list of customers and potential buyers. Send out newsletters featuring product updates, promotions, and exclusive offers.

If you have a physical store or participate in craft fairs, you can integrate your Etsy marketing efforts. Ensure your branding remains consistent across all platforms, whether online or offline. Your logo, colors, and messaging should be uniform. Encourage customers from your physical store to follow you on social media or subscribe to your email list for updates and special offers.

Promote your Etsy shop in your physical store or at craft fairs. Provide business cards or flyers with your Etsy shop information to interested customers.

Marketing your Etsy shop is an exciting journey filled with creative opportunities. Remember that success takes time, and each effort you put in brings you closer to your goals. With the right strategies, a well-managed budget, and a passion for your craft, your Etsy shop can flourish, connecting you with customers who appreciate your unique creations.

CHAPTER 6:
INVENTORY
MANAGEMENT

B efore you go too far in building your Etsy shop, you'll probably want to figure out what to do when something sells! Beyond shipping it out and getting paid, that is. Do you immediately need to backfill the space? Should you do it in groups? Is there a best practice to follow?

Because you paid close attention to the "Product Mix" discussion in Chapter 2, you know that digital inventory manages itself, which means you have no worries when a digital product sells. But physical inventory is different.

Shelf Life

If a product sits in your shop for a year and doesn't sell, should it stay there? What is the right amount of time a product should be in your shop before it sells? Do customer favorites eventually convert to sales?

Deciding how long to list a product on Etsy before pulling it from your shop inventory requires a strategic approach to shelf life. Etsy's algorithm favors fresh inventory, so you'll have to rotate your stock monthly or more often to remain high in the listings. Consider these factors when deciding whether to pull a product from inventory, or stock more of a particular product.

Regularly review the performance of each listing, including views, favorites, and sales. Analyze data from Etsy's seller dashboard or analytics tools to understand how well the product resonates with buyers. A product with a high favorite count that doesn't sell may need a price adjustment to become a steady seller. If you can maintain your profit margin, go for it! If not, consider taking the listing down.

Compare the performance of the product to your other listings. If it's significantly underperforming, it may be time to reconsider its presence in your inventory.

Consider the seasonality of the product and its relevance to current trends. Some items may experience fluctuations in demand throughout the year or may become outdated over time. You may want to pull the listings for winter items during spring and summer, and relist them in the fall, for example.

Likewise, holiday themed items have a limited appeal, so post and retire them thoughtfully. Just because a listing *can* last for four months doesn't mean it *should*. Does anyone buy Valentine's gifts in May?

Monitor trends in your niche market and adjust your inventory accordingly. If a product is no longer in high demand or no longer appears in other shops, it may be time to remove it from your shop.

Calculate the inventory turnover rate for each product, which measures how quickly the item sells relative to the amount of time it has been listed. A high turnover rate indicates strong demand and suggests that the item should remain in your inventory if it can be produced quickly enough to maintain desired inventory levels.

Use the turnover rate to prioritize which products to focus on and identify slow-moving items that may need to be removed from your inventory sooner.

Evaluate the profitability of each listing by considering factors such as the cost of materials, labor, and listing fees. Compare the revenue generated by the product to its associated costs to determine its overall profitability. Focus on products with healthy profit margins and consider removing listings that consistently yield low returns or result in losses.

Pay attention to customer feedback and reviews for each product. Positive reviews indicate satisfied customers and can help boost sales, while negative feedback may signal issues that need to be addressed. Items with negative feedback tend to sell more slowly, so a price adjustment may be in order, or you may want to pull the product entirely.

Use customer feedback to identify opportunities for product improvements or modifications. If a customer loves a feature on one product, consider pulling related products and adding that feature before relisting them.

Consider practical considerations such as storage space and production capacity. If a product occupies valuable storage space or requires significant resources to produce, it should justify its presence in your inventory through consistent sales and strong profitability.

Prioritize products that make efficient use of your resources and contribute positively to your overall business objectives.

By systematically evaluating these shelf life factors, you can make informed decisions about how long to list a product in your Etsy shop before deciding to remove it from your inventory.

Managing Vintage Items Inventory

Sourcing and managing vintage items inventory for your Etsy shop involves a combination of strategic sourcing, effective inventory management, and curation to maintain a cohesive theme. You may have an extensive collection of items you're planning to sell, or you may be starting from scratch. Either way, you'll need to continuously backfill to maintain an inventory. Here are some ideas for maintaining your inventory.

Sourcing Vintage Items

The time you spend sourcing your inventory items is an expense. Pay yourself a living wage for this time. Give each shopping trip a target amount of time and value sought. For example, 4 hours to collect $100 or merchandise that can be sold for $250 after cleaning and minor repairs. This is a business expense you can declare on your taxes! If you can systematically shop and source, you'll be able to keep your shop inventory consistent.

Keep a spreadsheet of how long it takes you to source how many dollars of inventory. Include the time it takes to prepare an item for sale – cleaning, repair, photography, etc.

Curate before you buy! Decide in advance which areas of your shop need some additional inventory, and only shop for those items. Your brand needs a consistent theme, personality, and pricing level. You don't want your shop to be an unrecognizable pile of unrelated products! If you decide you're shopping for Steampunk-friendly apparel, stick to it! You're shopping for work, not for pleasure!

Thrift Stores and Estate Sales: Visit local thrift stores, garage and rummage sales, estate sales, and flea markets to discover unique vintage pieces. I've found amazing pieces for pennies on the dollar. Carry cash, and haggle prices. Develop relationships with store owners and sellers to gain access to new inventory regularly. Many store owners will be happy to snap an image with their phone and send you a picture of an item if they believe you are likely to buy. It will save them time and effort cleaning and pricing an item!

Online Marketplaces: Explore online marketplaces like eBay, Craigslist, and Facebook Marketplace to find vintage items. Use search filters and alerts to track specific items or categories. Be careful here, as the prices tend to be higher, and may ruin your profit margin.

Networking: Connect with collectors, antique dealers, and other vintage sellers to source items through networking and referrals. Attend industry events, trade shows, and antique fairs to expand your sourcing network.

Effective Inventory Management

Categorize Inventory: Organize your vintage items into categories or themes, such as clothing, home decor, or collectibles, to streamline inventory management. Break it down further into season or holiday so you can tell at a glance what your inventory levels are for high sales periods.

Cataloging: Maintain detailed records of your inventory, including item descriptions, condition, pricing, and acquisition date. Tag by gender, genre, season, or holiday if applicable. Add any changes you made to the condition of the item, and how long it took you to make it sale ready. Use inventory management software or spreadsheets to track inventory levels and sales history of similar items.

Storage Solutions: Invest in storage solutions such as shelves, bins, or garment racks to organize and store vintage items efficiently. Vintage items can be very sensitive to the environment, including sunlight, temperature, and humidity. Proper storage helps preserve the condition of your inventory and facilitates easy access for fulfillment.

Curating A Cohesive Theme

Stay True to Your Niche: Identify a specific niche or theme for your vintage shop based on your interests, expertise, and target market. Then, stick to it! Don't make exceptions or your shop will be confusing. It's easy to forget that you're shopping for work, not your own personal taste, but the more you work that skill, the stronger it will get.

Consistent Aesthetic: Curate your inventory to maintain a consistent aesthetic or style within your chosen theme. Consider factors such as color palette, materials, and design elements to ensure cohesion across your listings.

Create Collections: Group related items together to create curated collections, specially priced bundles, or themed listings. When you're sourcing, you may find related items at the same yard sale or thrift store. Consider if this would make a great group, bundle, or collection! This makes it easier for customers to discover complementary pieces and encourages multiple purchases.

Regularly Refresh Inventory: Continuously source new inventory to keep your shop fresh and exciting. Rotate listings, introduce seasonal items, and highlight featured products to maintain customer interest and engagement. Remember, Etsy favors freshness to remain near the top of the search results.

Managing Handmade Goods Inventory

Managing inventory and crafting handmade goods, as opposed to drop shipped goods or digital goods, requires careful planning and organization. Drop shipped and digital products restock themselves, whereas handmade goods do not. You need to plan well to ensure smooth operations, timely order fulfillment, and customer satisfaction. Here are some best practices for your handmade stock.

Defining the time it takes to make an Etsy product and have it safely ready for shipping means understanding and timing your production process, including crafting time, processing time, and shipping preparation. You can create a timeline for yourself that should make it easier to know when you need to build more inventory for your shop. Follow these steps.

Analyze your production process. If you sell products made by others, you'll need to do this for their production, too, so you understand the lead time required to produce an item and prepare it for shipping.

Break down the production process into individual tasks required to create the product. This will include crafting or assembling the item, quality control checks, packaging, and labeling.

Time each task involved in the production process accurately. Consider factors such as the complexity of the item, the skill level required, and any potential interruptions or delays. Keep in mind that crafting time may vary depending on factors such as product customization, batch size, and your experience level. Add up the number of minutes involved, including any "wait" time, like drying time, cooling time, bonding time, etc. Include the time to photograph each item (if you make only unique items), and any photo editing time. This is your Time Per Unit.

How many units can you make per hour? Per workday? How many hours or days per week are you willing to create? Choose this answer carefully because you still have paperwork, shopping for materials, and shipping to do. Your total number of creating hours times the number of units per hour is your total Weekly Production Capacity.

At first you won't need to work to capacity because you're still building a following, but it's helpful to know what it is so that when your orders become steady, you'll know how to meet them.

Getting back to the handmade goods, you will find you are able to complete units more quickly and efficiently over time. Some makers can even double their speed! But with speed, there is the risk of making more mistakes.

Quality control matters! Before you package that item, look it over critically. Try to find mistakes, errors, and inconsistencies. It's better to find an error yourself than to ship it to a customer and have them find it! If speeding up you process is decreasing the quality of your product, slow down again until you can work quickly at a high quality.

Receiving Orders And Managing Lead Time

Define your lead time. Lead time refers to the time it takes from receiving an order to shipping it out. For custom handmade goods, lead time will include crafting time, processing time, and shipping time. For pre-completed goods, you will just need processing and shipping time.

Most successful Etsy sellers I've spoken with build in a 1 day lead time buffer for domestic orders, and a 2 day lead time buffer for international orders. This means that if your total lead time is 4 days before the buffer, you'll add the buffer time to the 4 days. Customers rarely complain if an item is delivered early, but often become frustrated if an item is received later than expected.

Prepare your item for shipping. Allocate time for packaging and preparing the individual product for shipping. Maybe all your items will take the same materials and time to package, but this is not usually the case. Selecting appropriate packaging materials, labeling the package with shipping labels and tracking information, and completing any necessary documentation takes time! Choose the ideal packaging protocol for each product, and make a note of it so you do it the same way each time. This is your Packaging Materials List. Find out how long it takes to wrap and package, and make a note of it. This is your Shipping Time Per Unit. You'll also want to weigh the completed, packaged item to learn your Total Shipping Weight.

If you choose to ship internationally, consider any additional steps required for international shipments, such as customs forms and regulations.

Items may sell faster than you can make them or source them, package them, and ship them. Good for you! You can raise your prices slightly, which will slow the speed of sales. But if you are consistently out of stock on popular items, you'll have a problem.

Remember what we discussed in Chapter 2 about your product mix in your inventory. Digital and drop shipped items never go out of stock, so if you incorporate them into your shop will never be completely empty. Just make sure you curate the items to go well with your defined brand.

Define realistic lead times based on the complexity of your products, your crafting capacity, inventory, holidays, and potential delays. Communicate lead times clearly on your Etsy shop to manage customer expectations and reduce the likelihood of disappointments.

Inventory Tracking Systems And Organization

Tips

What happens if you sell 3 of something that you only made 2 of? Oh NO! This is what inventory management is for. Managing inventory for an Etsy shop effectively requires a combination of organization, tracking, and analysis. While some sellers may prefer manual methods like spreadsheets, others may opt for specialized inventory management software. If you're in this for the long haul, I suggest the software, as it is faster and easier to scale. Here are some options for both.

Inventory Management Software:

CraftyBase is an inventory and bookkeeping system that integrates with Etsy, Shopify, and WooCommerce. CraftyBase is specifically designed for businesses that are run by makers and crafters. It allows you to keep track of your crafting and shipping materials in addition to completed inventory items. Super helpful!

Zoho Inventory Manage your online business with a comprehensive inventory and order management system. Zoho Inventory integrates with popular ecommerce platforms Etsy, eBay, and Amazon, as well as marketplaces like Shopify. Fulfill all orders across platforms with this centralized system.

Sellbrite: An all-in-one multichannel selling platform that includes inventory management, order fulfillment, and listing management for Etsy Amazon, Shopify, eBay, WooCommerce and other marketplaces. One stop shopping may be your easiest answer. And as of this writing, Sellbrite advertises itself as FREE for businesses processing fewer than 30 orders per month. In your first year of Etsy business, this is probably you!

Spreadsheets:

Google Sheets or Microsoft Excel: Both are versatile tools for creating custom inventory management systems. If you don't know how to use them, there are free tutorials inside the tools as well as all over YouTube. You've got this! Here's how you could structure a basic spreadsheet:

Create separate sheets for inventory items (merchandise, shipping materials, and crafting materials can each have their own page), sales orders, and suppliers.

Include columns for item name, SKU, quantity on hand, reorder point, supplier information, and cost. You may also want to include columns for lead time, and total shipping weight.

Use formulas to calculate total inventory value, reorder quantities, and profit margins.

Set up conditional formatting to highlight low stock levels or upcoming reorder dates.

Update the spreadsheet with all sales and inventory adjustments to maintain accuracy.

You can also explore templates available online or customize existing templates to suit your needs. There are lots of them! Start with a Google search for the exact type of information you are trying to manage.

When selecting inventory management software or creating a spreadsheet, consider factors such as your budget, the complexity of your inventory needs, scalability, and ease of use. Whichever method you choose, maintaining accurate inventory records is important for optimizing stock levels, reducing fulfillment errors, and providing a positive customer experience on Etsy. Look them all over, and choose what seems most intuitive to you.

Managing Your Stock

Shelf stock (completed items) and materials must be managed to keep your production of items steady. Keep a well-organized inventory of raw materials and finished products to avoid stockouts and production delays. This includes your shipping materials! If you don't have them on hand, you'll have to add shopping time for materials every time you want to ship an item. Don't make this mistake! It's time consuming, and expensive.

At first, it may be tempting to buy or source items in bulk to eliminate delays and take advantage of bulk pricing, but I suggest you wait and monitor your shop traffic before you buy in large volume. Some materials don't age well! And all that material requires storage, as will your completed inventory items. Make sure you don't overcrowd yourself. (Avoid closet avalanches, and garages you can't walk in. Take it from me!)

Buy what you need to create and ship your first 20-50 items – no more! After you've been selling for 4-6 months you'll have a better idea of how much inventory you need to keep on hand.

Establish relationships with reliable suppliers to ensure a steady supply of materials. Monitor inventory levels to reorder materials before running out. Learn how long acquiring materials should take, and order slightly more than you need to account for spillage, errors, etc. Regularly assess demand trends and adjust stock levels accordingly. Consider factors like seasonal variations, trends, and popular items.

Categorize and label materials and finished products for easy identification and access. Consider using shelving, bins, or containers to keep items organized. Many makers organize by materials (all the paint together) or by purpose (all the tools together). Others organize by product (everything to make product 1.) Find a process that is logical to you, and makes it easy to measure and record inventory of raw materials and finished items.

Implement a first-in, first-out (FIFO) approach to manage inventory turnover and reduce the risk of spoilage or obsolescence. That means new stock goes to the back or bottom of your supply, so you use the oldest materials first. In this way your stock will be in constant rotation and remain fresh.

Conduct regular inventory audits to reconcile physical stock with recorded quantities and identify any discrepancies or potential issues. If you're anything like me, you'll find you have some blind spots. For me, it's tape and pens. I never remember to write them into inventory until I audit!

Dealing with Seasonal Variations in Demand

After your first year, you'll be happy to have some great records to help you organize future years. Analyze past sales data to identify seasonal patterns and anticipate fluctuations in demand.

Plan production schedules and stock levels accordingly, ramping up production during peak seasons and scaling back during slower periods.

Consider offering seasonal promotions or themed collections to capitalize on seasonal trends and attract customers. Equally, this will allow you to clear out older inventory by bundling or reducing prices. It's always better to clear old inventory during an otherwise trending promotion. Frequent off-cycle discounting can make your inventory seem like it's of lower value.

Overall, successful inventory management, sourcing, and handmade goods production for your shop requires careful planning, efficient organization, and the flexibility to adapt to changing sales levels. It's not complicated. None of the steps are hard, but there are a lot of steps. Just follow them in order, like driving a car or baking a cake, and it will work out.

By implementing these best practices, you can streamline

operations, optimize inventory levels, and deliver exceptional customer experiences.

CHAPTER 7:
PACKAGING AND
SHIPPING SUCCESS

Y ou've made or sourced a wonderful product, and your customer has ordered! Hooray! Your next opportunity to make a great impression on your customer is through your packaging.

Packaging plays a vital role in the overall customer experience and branding for you as an Etsy seller. Just like opening a gift on a special occasion, opening your Etsy item can delight your customer, or frustrate them. Simple touches like colored tissue paper, fragranced packing peanuts, cloth ribbons, or a personalized note make customers feel valued, and enhance the perceived value of your product. Too much tape, an item that is difficult to open, or a broken item decrease perceived value.

Complimentary reviews that mention excellent shipping give buyers confidence that their item will arrive in good shape, which increases sales. It's well worth taking a moment to package your items with care.

Depending on the price point of your item, a higher-end package may be expected. The more expensive your product is in relation to the average price of a competing product, the more important beautiful, secure packaging will be.

Packaging Options And Details

Packaging is an additional cost above and beyond the cost of your item. In your shipping and handling pricing you can choose to list your actual cost, or you can blend some or all of it into the cost of your item. Make sure you're accounting for this additional cost somewhere!

Choose Appropriate Packaging: Select packaging materials that provide adequate protection for your products while aligning with your brand aesthetic. Options include padded envelopes, corrugated cardboard boxes, bubble mailers, or eco-friendly packaging materials like recycled paper or biodegradable mailers.

Size and Dimensions: Optimize packaging size to minimize shipping costs while ensuring that items fit securely without excessive movement. Consider using adjustable packaging solutions, like envelopes, to accommodate various product sizes.

Branding Elements: Incorporate branding elements such as logos, stickers, or branded tape to personalize the packaging and enhance brand recognition. Customized packaging inserts, thank-you notes, or business cards can also add a personal touch to the unboxing experience.

Get Imaginative: Imaginative packaging materials and inserts can elevate the unboxing experience for customers, leaving a lasting impression and reinforcing brand identity. Here are some creative options to consider:

Color Coordinate

If your brand or item has a specific color theme, feature it in your packaging. Use colored packaging paper, colored stickers or tape, and colored ribbon to secure your item.

Eco-Friendly Materials

Seed Paper: Plantable seed paper can be embedded with seeds that customers can plant after use, promoting sustainability and green initiatives. It's great paper to use for your Thank You note!

Recycled Materials: Choose packaging materials made from recycled paper, cardboard, or biodegradable plastics to minimize environmental impact. Make a note of it on the outside of your package. (Shipped in 100% post-consumer recycled packaging.)

Mushroom Packaging and Biodegradable Peanuts: Mushroom-based packaging materials, made from mycelium, are biodegradable and can be molded into various shapes to protect products during shipping. Other biodegradables include PLA, and materials made from popcorn and cornstarch.

Natural and Organic Elements

Twine or Raffia: Use natural twine or raffia to tie packages together instead of traditional plastic or synthetic ribbons. This adds a rustic and eco-friendly touch to the packaging.

Dried Flowers or Potpourri: Include dried flowers or potpourri as decorative elements inside the package or as part of a packaging insert. This adds a botanical aesthetic and enhances the unboxing experience with beauty and fragrance.

Customized Packaging Inserts

Encourage customers to leave reviews by including Thank-You Notes. Include a personalized thank-you note or message inside the package expressing gratitude for the customer's purchase and encouraging them to share their feedback. Provide clear instructions on how to leave a review on your Etsy storefront.

Incentives and Discounts: Offer incentives such as discount codes or exclusive offers for customers who leave reviews on their purchases. Offer additional discounts for customers who leave a review on social media and tag you in the post. This encourages engagement and motivates customers to share their experiences.

Custom Stickers or Labels: Design custom stickers or labels

featuring your logo, brand name, or a personalized message to seal packages or adorn packaging materials.

Handwritten Notes: Include handwritten thank-you notes or messages expressing gratitude for the customer's purchase and encouraging them to share their experience in social media posts and writing a review.

Product Care Instructions: Provide detailed product care instructions or usage tips on a branded insert card to educate customers and enhance their experience with the product.

QR Codes: Include QR codes linking to exclusive content, behind-the-scenes footage, or tutorials related to the product to engage customers further and add value to their purchase.

DIY Kits: If applicable, include DIY kits or crafting supplies along with the main product to encourage creativity and extend the customer's interaction with your brand.

Interactive Packaging

Puzzle Boxes: Design packaging that doubles as a puzzle or interactive game, providing entertainment and engagement for customers as they unbox their purchase.

Pop-Up Cards: Create pop-up cards or inserts featuring intricate designs or messages related to your brand or product, adding a surprise element to the unboxing experience.

Origami or Paper Crafts: Incorporate origami or paper craft elements into the packaging design if they suit your product or your brand. Include folded paper animals, flowers, or geometric shapes to delight and entertain customers.

Themed Packaging

Seasonal Themes: Design packaging materials tailored to specific seasons or holidays, incorporating festive colors, motifs, and decorations to evoke a sense of celebration and joy. A few rubber stamps that you use to print designs on your shipping paper can make an inexpensive but noticeable difference!

Brand Storytelling: Use packaging to tell the story of your brand or product, incorporating illustrations, quotes, or anecdotes that resonate with your target audience and reinforce brand values.

Personalizing Packaging at a Low Cost

DIY Branding: Create custom labels, stickers, or stamps featuring your logo or brand name using affordable online printing services or DIY methods. This allows you to personalize packaging without significant expenses.

Creative Inserts: Design and print personalized inserts or thank-you notes using inexpensive cardstock, letterhead, or paper. Include a handwritten message to add a personal touch and strengthen the connection with customers.

Repurpose Materials: Explore creative ways to reuse or repurpose packaging materials to reduce costs and minimize environmental impact. For example, use leftover fabric scraps or newspaper as eco-friendly cushioning material. Just make sure to make it attractive. If using newspaper, remember that it leaves ink smudges on hands, and possibly product, so insulate your product with at least 2 layers of tissue paper or other paper lining.

By experimenting with these imaginative packaging materials and inserts, you can create memorable unboxing experiences that delight customers and leave a lasting impression, ultimately fostering brand loyalty and positive word-of-mouth.

Shipping

Quality shipping is essential for Etsy sellers because it directly impacts customer satisfaction, brand reputation, and repeat business. While it may be tempting to ship in the cheapest packaging and by the cheapest method, that's not what customers want. They're used to secure, trackable overnight, or even same day shipping from Amazon, Wal-Mart and Target! Here's why quality shipping matters and what customers consider to be good quality shipping.

Customers expect their orders to arrive within the estimated delivery window or earlier, and they expect it to be soon. Delays can lead to frustration and disappointment.

Customers value products that are securely packaged to prevent damage during transit. Fragile items should be adequately cushioned to ensure they arrive intact.

Providing tracking information allows customers to monitor the status of their shipment and anticipate its arrival, enhancing transparency and peace of mind. Some customers will check on their package regularly if they ordered a little late for the intended occasion, and they expect to be able to track the package.

Keeping customers informed about order status, shipping delays, or any issues that may arise demonstrates transparency and proactive customer service. It increases trust in you by your customers if they don't feel like they're in the dark.

High-quality shipping reflects positively on the seller's professionalism and attention to detail, contributing to a positive brand image. This is important as you build your reputation in the competitive retail space. Consistent shipping standards reinforce brand identity and build trust with customers, encouraging repeat purchases and referrals.

Reduce your return rate! Properly packaged and accurately delivered orders are less likely to result in returns due to damage or dissatisfaction, saving time and resources for both the seller and the customer.

Weighing and Labeling

It often makes sense for Etsy sellers to weigh and label their packages at home. This approach can save time and money compared to going to a post office or shipping center for each shipment. By preparing packages at home, sellers can streamline their shipping process, accurately calculate shipping costs, and have greater control over packaging materials. This takes some equipment. Here are some tools I recommend.

Postal Scale: A reliable postal scale is essential for accurately weighing packages. Look for a scale that can measure weights up to the maximum expected for your packages, typically between 10-50 pounds. Digital scales are preferable for their accuracy and ease of use.

Label Printer: A label printer allows sellers to print shipping labels directly from their computer, saving time and eliminating the need for handwritten labels. Thermal label printers are popular for their efficiency and cost-effectiveness. Models such as the DYMO LabelWriter or the Rollo Label Printer are commonly used by Etsy sellers.

Shipping Labels: Purchase adhesive shipping labels compatible with your label printer. These labels should adhere securely to packages and withstand handling during transit. Many label printers come with proprietary label rolls, but sellers can also purchase compatible labels from third-party suppliers.

Packing Materials: Stock up on packing materials such as boxes, bubble mailers, packing tape, bubble wrap, and packing peanuts. Choose packaging materials appropriate for the size and fragility of your products to ensure they arrive safely to customers.

Shipping Software: Consider using shipping software or integrations provided by Etsy to streamline the shipping process further. Shipping software can automate label creation, provide discounted shipping rates, and track shipments, saving sellers time and money.

Choosing and Printing Shipping Labels

Shipping labels make your packages go where they need to go. Printing shipping labels provides the shipper with a label that is easy to read, and the customer with a better experience. Print your labels. It saves time and inaccuracies in delivery, and it looks more professional.

Shipping Software Integration: Utilize shipping software like ShipStation, Pirate Ship, or Etsy's built-in shipping labels feature to generate and print shipping labels seamlessly. These platforms offer discounted shipping rates, batch processing, and integration with major carriers.

Printer Compatibility: Ensure that your printer is compatible with the label size and format required by your shipping carrier. Invest in a reliable label printer or use adhesive label sheets compatible with your standard printer for crisp and professional-looking labels. This is important! A smudged label will result in shipping delays, or worse, a lost item.

Label Accuracy: Double-check shipping addresses and label details to avoid costly shipping errors or delivery delays. Include order numbers, tracking information, and return addresses for added convenience and security.

Navigating shipping challenges is a nightmare no one wants.

The easiest way to handle shipping is to avoid problems in the first place. The labeling advice should have you off to a good start. Follow the additional best practices below for the fewest shipping headaches.

Shipping Cost Management

Shipping is an additional cost, but it is manageable. Consider the price point of your product, and make your shipping decisions accordingly. Sometimes it will make sense to choose more expensive shipping options, like insurance. Use your best judgment.

Research Shipping Providers: Explore various shipping carriers (e.g., USPS, FedEx, UPS, DHL) to compare rates, delivery times, and services offered. Many carriers offer discounted rates for businesses, which can help reduce costs. Familiarize yourself with all the services available, like hand-cancelling for fragile items. You'll be protecting your product and your customers.

Utilize Shipping Software: Invest in shipping software like ShipStation or Pirate Ship to streamline the shipping process. These platforms allow you to compare rates, print labels, and track shipments efficiently.

Packaging Efficiency: Optimize packaging to minimize

dimension and weight charges and ensure the safety of your products during transit. Consider using lightweight packaging materials without compromising on protection.

Offer Shipping Discounts: Providing free shipping or offering discounted shipping rates can attract more customers, or to retain existing ones. You can incorporate shipping costs into your product pricing or set minimum order thresholds for free shipping. You may want to offer this only at certain times of year, as a premium. The details are up to you!

Standard vs. Expedited Shipping: Provide customers with different shipping options to cater to their preferences and urgency. Offer standard shipping for cost-conscious buyers and expedited shipping for those who need their orders quickly. There will always be customers who buy at the last minute! Bailing them out of a jam earns loyalty.

Package Tracking: Always opt for shipping services that include tracking to provide customers with visibility into their order's delivery status. This helps reduce inquiries and improves customer satisfaction. Inquiries can take up an enormous amount of time without tracking!

Consider Shipping Insurance: Evaluate the need for shipping insurance, especially for high-value or fragile items. While it adds to the shipping cost, it provides financial protection in case of lost or damaged shipments. It will protect both you and your buyer. You get paid by the shipper, and you return the customer's money.

Handling International Shipping And Customs

If you choose to ship internationally, I suggest you choose no more than 2 nations outside of your own country to begin. As you learn how frequently you receive international requests, you may want to expand to more nations, or withdraw international shipping entirely.

Research International Shipping Regulations: Familiarize yourself with the customs regulations and import/export requirements of the countries you plan to ship to. Each country has its own set of rules regarding prohibited items, import duties, and taxes. They change periodically, so check for updates at least every 6 months or more.

Declare Accurate Values: Ensure that you accurately declare the value of the items being shipped on customs forms. Misdeclaring values can lead to delays, fines, or seizure of the shipment by customs authorities.

Provide Clear Shipping Policies: Clearly communicate international shipping policies, including estimated delivery times, potential customs fees, and import taxes, on your

Etsy storefront. This helps manage customer expectations and reduces misunderstandings.

Offer International Shipping Options: Consider expanding your customer base by offering international shipping. Consider using international shipping services provided by major carriers or third-party logistics providers to streamline the process and obtain competitive rates.

By implementing these packaging and shipping strategies, you can effectively navigate shipping challenges, reduce costs, and provide a delightful unboxing experience for your customers. In a nutshell, both will contribute to the growth and success of your businesses.

CHAPTER 8:
PHOTOGRAPHY
FOR ETSY

I n the world of Etsy, where visual appeal is paramount, product photography plays a pivotal role in attracting customers and driving sales. It's where artisans and creators showcase their unique goods to their online audience. It's how shoppers decide what to buy. As of this writing, Etsy allows up to 10 product images per listing. If your images are good, this is often more than you need! The trick is to make every image count.

In this chapter I'll delve into the *basics* of photographing items for Etsy, covering everything from equipment and setup to lighting techniques, styling tips, and post-processing tricks. This is not an advanced explanation, and I am not a professional photographer. These are fundamentals that have been effective for me in online selling.

Whether you're a seasoned seller looking to elevate your product photography game or a newcomer seeking to make a splash on the platform, this guide will help you improve your images. Try some ideas, and see what you think!

Essential Equipment

While you don't need a professional studio setup to capture stunning product photos for Etsy, having the right equipment can make a significant difference in the quality of your images. There is some essential gear you'll need, from cameras and lenses to tripods, backdrops, and props. We'll also explore the pros and cons of different camera types, such as DSLRs, mirrorless cameras, and smartphones, and provide tips for maximizing the capabilities of whatever equipment you have at your disposal.

Cameras And Equipment

DSLRs (Digital Single-Lens Reflex):

Pros: These are what most people have now, usually referred to as digital cameras. DSLRs offer excellent image quality, interchangeable lenses, manual controls, and versatility for various photography needs. They often have larger sensors, which can result in better image detail and low-light performance.

Cons: DSLRs can be bulkier and heavier than other camera types, which may be less convenient for on-the-go shooting. They can also have a steeper learning curve for absolute beginners.

Mirrorless Cameras:

Pros: Mirrorless cameras are more compact and lightweight than DSLRs, making them easier to carry and handle. They often feature advanced autofocus systems, electronic viewfinders, and 4K video capabilities.

Cons: While mirrorless cameras offer excellent image quality, their battery life may be shorter compared to DSLRs. They also have a more limited selection of lenses and accessories, although this is continually improving.

Smartphones:

Pros: Smartphones are incredibly convenient and accessible, allowing you to capture high-quality images quickly and easily. Many smartphones feature advanced camera technologies, such as multiple lenses, AI scene recognition, and built-in editing tools. Plus, you probably have one in your pocket right now!

Cons: While smartphones can produce impressive results, they may not offer the same level of control or image quality as dedicated cameras, especially in challenging lighting conditions. They also have limitations in terms of focal length, aperture control, and manual settings. If you must start with a smartphone, use a tripod, and follow the instructions for lighting and composition closely.

Lenses:

For product photography, I recommend starting with a versatile lens such as a prime lens (e.g., 50mm) or a zoom lens (e.g., 24-70mm) is ideal. Prime lenses typically offer wider apertures, allowing for beautiful background blur (bokeh) and low-light performance. Zoom lenses provide flexibility for framing and composition, especially when shooting products of varying sizes.

Tripods:

A sturdy tripod is essential for maintaining stability and preventing camera shake, especially when shooting in low light or using slow shutter speeds. This allows for ideal focus in nearly all situations. Look for a tripod with adjustable height, a ball head for precise positioning, and quick-release plates for easy setup and breakdown. Use it! It may seem strange at first, but I promise, it will become your best friend!

Backdrops:

Choose backdrops that complement your products without distracting from them. Seamless paper or fabric backgrounds in neutral colors such as white, gray, or black are versatile options. You can buy professional backdrops or use a solid white or gray wall or bed sheet. Place the object so that only the object and backdrop are visible in the image.

For beginners I suggest avoiding textured backgrounds, as they can distract from the product and its unique materials and texture. Consider a very few simple props that add visual interest and context to your product photos.

Props

A limited number of simple props can help tell a story and enhance the visual appeal of your product photos. Choose props that are relevant to your products and align with your brand aesthetic. For example, if you're selling handmade jewelry, you might use natural elements like leaves or stones as props to create a rustic, organic vibe. Make sure the product is the hero in your image!

Lighting

Effective lighting techniques and equipment are key for achieving high-quality product photography for Etsy. Here's a breakdown of some fundamental lighting techniques and the equipment you'll need.

Natural Light: Natural light can produce beautiful, soft illumination that enhances the appearance of your products. Position your setup near a window or door where soft, diffused light enters the room. If the weather permits, take images outdoors.

Avoid direct sunlight, which can create harsh shadows and overexposure. Instead, opt for indirect or filtered light that provides even illumination. Early morning and late afternoon provide beautiful light. Using a fill flash can help you eliminate shadows.

Use sheer curtains or diffusers to soften harsh sunlight and minimize glare. You can also use white foam boards or reflectors to bounce light onto shadowed areas and fill in shadows.

Continuous Lighting: Continuous lighting setups consist of artificial light sources that remain illuminated throughout the shoot. They provide consistent, predictable lighting conditions and are ideal for beginners.

Softbox lights are popular choices for product photography due to their diffused, even illumination. They help minimize harsh shadows and create flattering lighting for your products. They are particularly popular for small objects like jewelry and fishing lures, but come in a variety of sizes. They can be easily researched online. You can build your own, or buy one inexpensively.

LED panel lights offer adjustable brightness and color temperature, allowing you to customize the lighting to suit your preferences. They're energy-efficient and produce little heat, making them suitable for extended shooting sessions. Prices range from very inexpensive to thousands. Carefully evaluate your needs after you've tried working without them. If you need them, they can be purchased at most camera stores and online.

Studio Strobes/Flash: Studio strobes require more advanced knowledge and experience to use effectively compared to continuous lighting setups. They're also more expensive and may not be necessary for beginners or small-scale Etsy sellers.

Studio strobes or flash units provide powerful bursts of light that freeze motion and allow for faster shutter speeds. They're commonly used in professional studio settings for product photography. While your product is probably not in motion, they make most images appear very crisp.

When using studio strobes, you'll typically set up one or more lights and modify their intensity and direction using modifiers such as softboxes, umbrellas, or reflectors.

Lighting Accessories: Light modifiers such as softboxes, umbrellas, and reflectors help control the direction, intensity, and quality of light. Softboxes diffuse light to create soft, flattering shadows, while umbrellas spread light evenly for broader coverage. Reflectors bounce light back onto the subject to fill in shadows and add dimension. Using them can save you money on additional lighting!

Reflectors can be made at home for very little money. Research this on the internet, and you'll find hundreds of creative ideas!

Tips For Effective Lighting: Position your light source(s) at a 45-degree angle to the product to create soft, even illumination and minimize shadows. If you need an additional angle of the product, move the item, not the lighting.

Use a combination of key light (main light source), fill light (secondary light source to fill in shadows), and backlight (light placed behind the product to separate it from the background) for balanced lighting. Remember, these lighting effects are important to help your buyer see your product accurately. It will make the quality of your item more obvious! Deep shadows do not look professional.

Experiment with different lighting setups and angles to achieve the desired look for your products. Consider the mood and style you want to convey and adjust your lighting accordingly.

White Balance: Pay attention to the white balance settings on your camera to ensure accurate color representation in your product photos. You can set white balance manually based on the lighting conditions or use auto white balance for convenience. If your white balance is off, whites will have a color to them. This means all of the colors in your image are distorted. When the buyer sees them online, they won't see the real color of the item.

Avoid mixed lighting sources with different color temperatures, as this can result in color casts and inconsistent color rendering. All your lighting should be daylight balanced. Most light bulbs are not, so ensure that you're using consistent lighting to avoid distorting color and shadow depth.

Tips For Maximizing Equipment

Regardless of the equipment you have, focus on mastering basic photography principles such as composition, lighting, and exposure. Developing skill in these fundamentals will allow you to create compelling images regardless of your gear. The best gear won't make up for bad basic skills.

Experiment with different camera settings and shooting techniques to maximize the capabilities of your equipment. Learn how to adjust aperture, shutter speed, and ISO to achieve the desired exposure and depth of field.

Take advantage of natural light whenever possible, as it can produce beautiful, flattering results. Position your products near windows or doorways to harness soft, diffused light, or use reflectors and diffusers to control harsh shadows and highlights.

Invest in quality lenses and accessories that complement your shooting style and cater to your specific needs as a photographer. While it's tempting to splurge on the latest gear, prioritize items that will have the most significant impact on your photography.

Composition

Understanding Your Product

Before you even pick up your camera, it's crucial to understand the product you're photographing. Whether it's handmade jewelry, vintage clothing, or artisanal ceramics, each item has its unique features, textures, and selling points. Consider what makes your product true to the niche: color, age, size, materials, texture, specific uses, mood... Whatever it is that makes the product special, and defines the niche, should be showcased together to make the product jump of the screen to your buyer.

For every product, make a list of the most important aspects of your product, and note how you can tell that story visually. This will help you make every product image unique. If you don't, all your products may have a flat presence on screen that doesn't resonate with your customers.

Basic Techniques

By applying composition techniques thoughtfully, you can create images that not only showcase your products but also engage viewers and convey a narrative. Some may resonate with you, while others may not suit your style or products. Don't worry! Use what makes sense to you.

In the image below, you'll see images that are called "Golden Proportions." All of them are highly effective ways to position your focal point (your product) in a rectangular image. The top two, "Fibonacci focus" and the "rule of thirds," are the most commonly used in commercial product photography. This means that objects are composed in the image to draw your eye into the focal point in a structured way. It's in the smallest full rectangle in the "Fibonacci focus," and in any one of the full length thirds in the "rule of thirds." Both make positioning your product and your props and background interest easy!

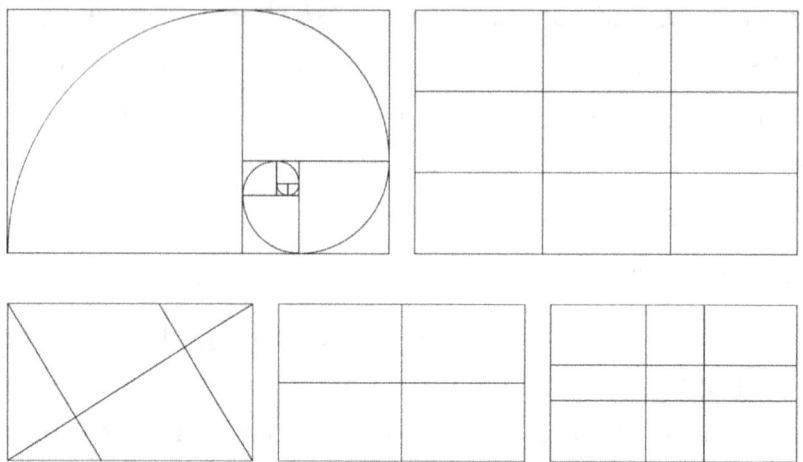

Focal Points: Establishing a clear focal point is essential for guiding the viewer's eye and drawing attention to the most important elements of the image. Use techniques such as selective focus, shallow depth of field, or contrasting colors and textures to make your product stand out against the background. Avoid cluttering the frame with distracting elements that compete for attention and detract from the focal point. Minimal props or competing textures make focal points more effective.

Rule of Thirds: The rule of thirds is a fundamental composition guideline that divides the frame into a grid of nine equal sections using two horizontal and two vertical lines. Placing the subject or key elements of the image along these lines or at their intersections can create a more balanced and visually appealing composition. This technique adds interest and dynamism to your photos by breaking away from the centered composition and encouraging viewers to explore the entire frame. Only use this technique in shots that show context of how the product is used, or lifestyle shots. Do not do this when your item is alone in the image, as it will look like a mistake!

Leading Lines: Leading lines are lines within the image that lead the viewer's eye towards the focal point or main subject. These lines can be literal, such as roads, paths, or architectural elements, or implied, such as patterns, shapes, or shadows. These can be very effective in creating mood and emotion. Incorporating leading lines into your composition helps create depth and visual flow, guiding the viewer's gaze through the image and emphasizing the product's importance.

Negative Space: Negative space, or empty space around the subject, can be used to create balance, emphasize the product, or evoke a sense of minimalism and simplicity. Leaving room for negative space allows the viewer's eye to rest and provides breathing room within the composition. If you fill the frame entirely with your item, it looks like an accident. Experiment with negative space to achieve a clean, uncluttered look that highlights your product effectively.

Symmetry and Asymmetry: Symmetry can create a sense of harmony and balance in your composition, while asymmetry can add visual interest and dynamism. Depending on your product and brand aesthetic, you can choose to emphasize symmetry for a more formal and structured look or embrace asymmetry for a more organic and spontaneous feel. You can create either effect by how you position your object on your background or in your scene. Pay attention to the placement of elements within the frame and experiment with different compositions to find what works best for your product.

Framing: Framing involves using elements within the image to frame the subject and draw attention to it. This can include natural frames such as doorways, windows, or foliage, as well as artificial frames like arches or props. By framing your product creatively, you can add depth and context to the image, inviting viewers to focus on the subject within the frame. It's important to use framing in the context of the regular use of the product, as it can convey size, color, and texture in unique ways.

Perspective: Perspective refers to the angle from which the photo is taken relative to the subject. Experimenting with different perspectives can dramatically alter the mood and perception of your product. For example, shooting from a low angle can make the product appear larger and more imposing, while shooting from above can create a sense of intimacy or vulnerability. Different emotions will work well with, or contrast against your brand. Play with perspective to evoke specific emotions or highlight different aspects of your product.

Storytelling

Using the dynamics of storytelling in product photography involves going beyond simply showcasing the item and instead crafting a visual narrative that engages the viewer emotionally and communicates the value and benefits of the product.

Leverage these storytelling techniques to create compelling product images.

Establish a Theme or Concept: Start by identifying a theme or concept that aligns with your brand identity and resonates with your target audience, based on the notes you took above. This could be a lifestyle, a mood, or a specific scenario that evokes a desired emotional response. For example, if you're selling handmade candles, your theme could revolve around relaxation and self-care.

Create a Setting or Environment: Set the stage by creating a context or environment that enhances the storytelling aspect of your product photography. This could involve selecting appropriate props, backgrounds, and lighting to convey the desired mood or atmosphere. What's key here is that the product is clearly defined, and not mistaken for one of the props! For instance, if you're selling outdoor camping gear, you might stage your products in a natural setting near rustic props like tents and campfires. Set the product apart, but have the props visible in the background of at least one image.

Focus on the Product's Use or Benefit: Showcasing how the product fits into the customer's life and addresses their needs or desires is key to effective storytelling in product photography. Instead of only displaying the product on its own, include an image that demonstrates its practical use or highlights its unique features and benefits. This could involve showing the product in action or illustrating the positive impact it can have on the customer's life. Moisturizing skin care could be photographed with "dew" drops on the packaging, for example.

Evoke Emotion: Emotions play a powerful role in storytelling, so aim to evoke feelings of joy, nostalgia, excitement, or aspiration in your product images. This could be achieved through the use of expressive models, evocative lighting, or relatable scenarios that resonate with your target audience. For example, if you're selling children's toys, you might capture the joy and wonder on a child's face as they play with the product.

Tell a Story Through Composition: Pay attention to composition techniques such as framing, perspective, and focal points to tell a story visually. Consider the flow of the image and how it guides the viewer's eye through the scene, leading them to focus on key elements of the narrative. People tend to view images from upper left to lower right, but you can change this. Faces often draw attention, as do bright colors. Experiment with different angles and viewpoints to create visual interest and convey the desired message effectively.

Include Supporting Elements: Supporting elements such as text overlays, captions, or lifestyle imagery can further enhance the storytelling aspect of your product photography. Use these elements strategically to reinforce the narrative (like pointing out where different materials are used), highlight key features or benefits (like size or motion), and encourage engagement with the viewer.

Maintain Consistency Across Your Brand: Consistency is key to effective storytelling in product photography, so ensure that your visual style, tone, and messaging are aligned with your brand identity across all channels. This helps to build brand recognition and establish a strong emotional connection with your audience over time.

Product Specifications

In many of your images, you'll want your product isolated on a plain background. This allows the buyer to focus on specifications they want to understand. In person, they can pick up an object to investigate color, weight, material, texture, and size. Online, they rely on the images you provide to understand your item.

Color: Accurate color representation is crucial in product photography, as it directly influences a buyer's perception of the item. To ensure color accuracy, it's essential to use proper lighting and white balance settings on your camera. Natural light or daylight-balanced artificial lighting produces the most accurate colors. It's essential to avoid oversaturation or color distortion, as this can mislead potential buyers and lead to dissatisfaction upon receipt of the product.

There is nothing you can do to ensure your buyers have accurately calibrated screens on which to assess your product, and some distortion will occur. Because of this, it's very important that the image you present is as close to accurate as possible.

Contrast: Contrast refers to the difference in brightness between the lightest and darkest parts of an image. Proper contrast helps create depth and dimensionality in product photos, making them visually engaging and dynamic. To enhance contrast, pay attention to lighting techniques such as using directional light to create shadows and highlights. Images with too little contrast appear flat and uninteresting. Adjusting exposure settings on your camera or during post-processing can also help fine-tune contrast levels. However, it's crucial to maintain a balance and avoid excessive contrast, which can lead to loss of detail and an unnatural appearance.

Texture: Texture adds tactile appeal to product images, allowing customers to visually experience the surface characteristics of the item. Whether it's the smooth finish of a ceramic mug or the intricate weave of a fabric, capturing texture accurately is essential for conveying the quality and craftsmanship of the product. To highlight texture, use diffused lighting to minimize harsh shadows and glare. Experiment with different angles and perspectives to showcase the surface details effectively. Close-up shots or macro photography can also be useful for emphasizing texture and inviting customers to explore the product more closely.

Ideal Backgrounds: The background serves as the canvas against which the product is showcased, and choosing the right background is crucial for highlighting the item itself. A clean, uncluttered background allows the product to stand out and keeps the focus on its features. Neutral backgrounds such as white, gray, or black are popular choices as they provide a versatile backdrop that complements a wide range of products without distracting from them. Alternatively, you can use textured backgrounds or props that enhance the product's aesthetic appeal and create a cohesive visual theme. When selecting a background, consider the product's color, shape, and size to ensure it enhances rather than detracts from the overall composition.

Styling Tips And Tricks

In product photography, styling plays a role in ensuring that the products are presented in the most visually appealing and engaging way possible. Styling helps to conceptualize, plan, and execute the visual aesthetic of the photoshoot. The goal is to present the product in a way that engages the customer while making the product integral to the lifestyle the brand represents. It's the difference between a scarf on a plain white backdrop and a scarf on a beautiful woman, running in the street in London, with a smile on her face and wind in her hair. Styling should occur in one or two of your shots for any lifestyle products.

Conceptualization and Planning: As we discussed earlier In the chapter, create a list of words that identify what you are trying to convey with your images. If you're photographing a whole collection or a high ticket item, develop creative concepts and mood boards to guide the styling direction, including color palettes, props, and overall aesthetic. It's easier to work this all out before you start photography!

Prop Styling: If you're using props select props and accessories that complement the products and enhance the overall visual storytelling. Ideally, some of your props can come from your shop! Arrange props in the scene to create a cohesive composition and add depth and context to the images. If a prop doesn't make the story clearer and stronger, skip it.

Set Design and Decoration: Create visually appealing sets or backgrounds that complement the products and convey the desired mood or theme. Consider elements such as lighting, textures, colors, and patterns to enhance the overall aesthetic of the scene. It is critically important that the set design and décor does not distract from the primary product. What looks great in person does not always read well in an image. Be ready to make some adjustments.

Styling Techniques and How-Tos:

Lighting, lighting, lighting! Before you change a layout, try several different types of lighting. You'll discover that more or less light, or redirecting light from another angle can highlight different features of your product. One layout can support dozens of images.

Use styling tools such as fabric clamps, tape, and adhesive putty to position products and props precisely within the scene. Just keep your tools out of sight of the camera. Do what you need to do to create the perfect image: iron fabric, tape something down so it doesn't move in a draft, etc. As long as you haven't changed the product, you're good.

Experiment with different arrangements, angles, and perspectives to find the most flattering and engaging compositions. You may have the right stuff in the wrong order to highlight what you want to about your item. Move things around!

Pay attention to details such as product positioning, alignment, and spacing to ensure a polished and professional appearance.

Here are some professional insider tips and tricks for styling different types of products to give you more ideas. There's even some guidance on incorporating props, color palettes, textures, and lifestyle elements to create compelling compositions!

Jewelry and Accessories: Use a variety of props such as jewelry stands, velvet or silk fabric, or decorative boxes to elevate your jewelry and accessories. High end jewelry should have rich colors and fabrics, while casual jewelry should have simpler fabrics and more moderate color. Use your props to enhance the mood and provide lifestyle context.

In a shot with necklaces or several pieces of jewelry, use height to showcase movement and texture. Place the top of a necklace at one level on one prop, and have the chain dangle down onto another one. Place a couple of bangles on one level, and a group of rings and earrings on another. Show what it might look like to own several pieces of your collection.

Experiment with different arrangements and compositions to showcase the unique features and details of each piece, such as layering necklaces or stacking bracelets.

Consider incorporating natural elements like flowers or leaves to add a touch of organic beauty to your compositions. Place pieces on unusual things, like fine furniture or granite. The textural contrast will make your pieces stand out.

Pay attention to lighting and reflections to highlight the sparkle and shine of gemstones or metals. Start with freshly polished and cleaned pieces, and use bright lighting.

Clothing: Use mannequins or models to showcase clothing items in a realistic and relatable way. Style hair/wigs and accessories to create a mood.

Pay attention to garment details such as seams, buttons, and textures, and use styling techniques such as folding or draping to highlight these features. Customers love to see the details, and if you don't show them, they may pass you by.

Experiment with different poses and angles to capture the silhouette and movement of the clothing. Does the garment have pleats on the sides or back? Show 'em. A neatly tucked waist? Show it! Amazing shaping? You need to show at least one front, back, and side image for garments that are not socks.

Outdoor shots should reflect the context of where the garment will be worn.

Background colors in images should make the colors in the garment appear sharp and appealing. Don't let your garment blend into the background!

Consider styling clothing items in context, such as pairing them with coordinating accessories or styling them for specific occasions or seasons.

Home Decor: Arrange home decor items in vignettes or styled scenes to create a sense of ambiance and lifestyle. Green potted plants always make good peripheral and background items.

Pay attention to scale and proportion when styling larger items such as furniture or artwork.

Experiment with layering textures and patterns to add depth and visual interest to your compositions. Just avoid any textures or patterns that will compete with your product as the focal point of the image.

Incorporate elements of interior design such as candles, art, furniture, or decorative objects to create a cohesive and inviting atmosphere.

Mastering product photography for Etsy is a journey that requires dedication, creativity, and a willingness to learn and adapt. By understanding your products, investing in the right equipment, and honing your technical skills, you can create stunning images that captivate customers and drive sales. Remember, photography is not just about capturing objects;

it's about telling stories, evoking emotions, and building connections with your audience. So pick up your camera, unleash your creativity, and let your products shine on Etsy and beyond.

CHAPTER 9:
EXPANDING
THE BUSINESS
(WITHOUT GETTING
OVERWHELMED)

E tsy has become home to your shop, where you showcase and sell your unique handmade and vintage products. While you're starting your Etsy shop, you should be considering what scaling it into a profitable and sustainable business will take. It requires strategic planning and execution. In this chapter, I'll explore five key strategies for sellers to scale their business on Etsy: diversifying the product mix, offering drop-ship items, hiring help, outsourcing tasks, and automating parts of the work. By considering these things from the beginning, you'll learn more from other makers about how they have grown their businesses because you'll know what to pay attention to!

Diversifying The Product Mix

As we discussed in Chapter 2, diversifying your product mix is a big step in establishing your Etsy business. It's a big part of scaling it, too! As time goes on, you'll want to be thinking of, and making a list of, all the products that might fit under your niche, and improve your shop. Expanding your range of offerings can attract a broader customer base and increase your revenue potential.

Start by conducting thorough market research and trend analysis to identify popular and trending product categories on Etsy. Use tools like Google Trends, Etsy's own search bar, and competitor research to spot emerging trends and customer preferences. Look for products that align with your brand and expertise while offering growth potential.

Once you've identified new product categories, consider adding complementary items to your existing lineup. Maintain a balance between existing products and new additions to ensure a cohesive brand identity. You don't want to change everything all at once! Gradually introduce new products to gauge their popularity and customer response.

Consider collaborating with other Etsy sellers or artisans to create unique product bundles or exclusive collections. For example, under the wedding heading, you could coordinate with a vendor of gift bags and packages for members of the wedding party.

If you haven't before, consider offering customization options to cater to individual customer preferences and create a personalized shopping experience.

Engage regularly with your audience to understand their needs and incorporate their feedback into new product offerings.

Offering Drop-Ship Items

It's crucial to review Etsy's policies regularly, as they may change. Violating Etsy's policies regarding drop shipping or other selling practices could result in your shop being shut down. Drop shipping is a popular way to scale an Etsy business without the need for significant inventory management or upfront costs. Here's how to integrate drop-shipping into your Etsy shop:

Research and select reputable drop shipping suppliers who offer quality products and reliable shipping. Consider how well the product aligns with your niche, and whether it will meet with your quality standards. Is there profit potential?

Read the reviews! Ensure that your chosen suppliers have a proven track record of delivering products on time and in good condition.

Set up a seamless integration between your Etsy shop and the drop shipping supplier's platform. Work with the drop shipper to beta test whether the integration is functional.

Use order automation tools to streamline the order placement process, reducing the risk of errors. Some popular third-party tools and platforms that integrate with Etsy for drop shipping include Inventory Source, Printful, and AOP+. These tools can help automate order processing, inventory management, and product syncing.

Print on Demand (POD) Services: Many Etsy sellers use print-on-demand services to create and fulfill custom designs on various products like t-shirts, mugs, or posters. These POD services integrate with Etsy and handle the production and shipping of products based on your designs and customer orders.

Clearly state that the product is a drop-shipped item and specify the estimated delivery time. It's important that your buyer understand this, both due to Etsy policy and in case there is a delay or damaged item.

Provide excellent customer service by promptly responding to inquiries and addressing concerns. Keep customers informed about the status of their orders and any potential delays. Handle returns and refunds professionally, even if the issue is with the supplier.

Hiring Help

As your Etsy business grows, you may find it challenging to

manage all aspects of your shop on your own. Hiring help can free up your time and expertise for more strategic tasks. Here's how to go about it:

Determine which aspects of your Etsy business can be delegated or require additional expertise. Common areas for hiring help include product creation, product photography, marketing, customer service, and bookkeeping. These are less creative drivers of the business, and more "nuts and bolts." Consider what is the most time consuming part of your work, and whether you are receiving the level of return you need. Often it is cheaper to hire help than to literally waste time on tasks you're not good at!

Consider hiring freelancers or independent contractors for specific tasks or projects. Use platforms like Upwork, Fiverr, or Freelancer to find qualified professionals in your chosen field. Clearly outline your expectations, deliverables, and payment terms in your contracts. When possible, start with a small test project. If you're happy with the quality of work, move to bigger projects.

Partner with other artisans or businesses to share responsibilities or resources. This can be particularly beneficial for co-creating products, cross-promotions, or sharing production space.

If your business experiences substantial growth, consider hiring part-time or full-time employees. Carefully assess the skills and qualifications required for each role and conduct interviews to find the right candidates. Ensure compliance with labor laws and provide appropriate training and support. If you've never had employees before, you'll want to consult with a business attorney for guidance on how to comply with local laws.

Outsourcing Tasks

Outsourcing is another effective way to scale your Etsy business, allowing you to focus on core activities while experts handle specialized tasks. It's different from hiring help, in that you'll be doing business with another business, not hiring an individual. Here's how to approach outsourcing:

Evaluate your daily, weekly, and monthly tasks to identify which ones can be outsourced. Common tasks suitable for outsourcing include bookkeeping, social media management, and SEO optimization.

Research and select reputable outsourcing providers, agencies, or virtual assistants with expertise in your required tasks. Ask friends, business associates, or members of your social network. Check references and reviews to ensure their reliability and professionalism.

Clearly define the scope of work, expectations, and deadlines in your outsourcing contracts. Make sure you understand what is included before you agree to a price. Include provisions for quality control and revisions if necessary.

Implement systems to monitor the progress and quality of outsourced tasks. Regularly review the work and provide feedback to maintain accountability.

Automating Parts Of The Work

Automation is a powerful tool for streamlining your Etsy business operations, reducing manual labor, and improving efficiency. Here's how to automate various aspects of your shop:

Use inventory management software to track stock levels and automatically update listings when products are low in stock. Set up alerts for reordering materials or products to avoid stockouts.

Some good ones to consider are:

TradeGecko: TradeGecko offers robust inventory management features, including order and stock level tracking, multi-channel selling integrations, and reporting tools. It also integrates with Etsy and can help you manage your Etsy shop's inventory efficiently.

InventoryLab: InventoryLab is designed for e-commerce sellers and provides features like real-time inventory tracking, cost of goods sold (COGS) calculations, and profit analysis. It can integrate with your Etsy shop to streamline inventory management.

Stitch Labs: Stitch Labs is known for its multichannel inventory management capabilities. It can help you synchronize inventory levels across various sales channels, including Etsy, and provide insights into your stock performance.

Zoho Inventory: Zoho Inventory is a user-friendly option that enables you to manage inventory, orders, and shipments. It integrates seamlessly with Etsy and offers a range of automation features.

Shopventory: Shopventory is designed for small businesses and offers real-time inventory tracking, sales analytics, and integrations with multiple sales channels, including Etsy.

Automating order processing, label creation, and tracking for Etsy shops can save you time and streamline your operations. While Etsy provides some basic order management features, integrating third-party tools can enhance the automation process. Here are some tools that can help automate order processing, label creation, and tracking for your Etsy shop:

ShipStation: ShipStation is a popular shipping and order fulfillment platform that integrates with Etsy. It allows you to automate order imports, create shipping labels, and track shipments across multiple carriers. ShipStation also provides tools for batch processing and custom packing slips.

Shippo: Shippo is an easy-to-use shipping and label creation tool that integrates with Etsy. It offers discounted shipping rates, batch label printing, and real-time tracking updates. Shippo also supports various carriers and offers international shipping solutions.

Etsy Shipping Labels: Etsy provides its own shipping label creation tool, which allows you to purchase and print shipping labels directly from your Etsy shop. While it may not have advanced automation features, it's convenient for sellers looking to simplify the shipping process.

Pirate Ship: Pirate Ship is a free shipping software that can integrate with Etsy. It offers simple and cost-effective label creation, including Priority Mail Cubic pricing. It's suitable for small and medium-sized Etsy sellers.

ShippingEasy: ShippingEasy is an order and shipping management platform that integrates with Etsy. It provides features like order syncing, label creation, batch processing, and order tracking. ShippingEasy also offers discounted shipping rates.

Ordoro: Ordoro is a multi-channel order and inventory management software that can connect with your Etsy shop. It offers order automation, label creation, and real-time tracking. It also supports multiple sales channels and inventory synchronization.

Aftership: Aftership specializes in shipment tracking and delivery notifications. While it may not create labels, it can help you track packages from multiple carriers and provide tracking updates to your customers automatically.

Multiorders: Multiorders is a multichannel inventory and order management platform that integrates with Etsy. It offers order processing automation, label creation, and real-time tracking. Multiorders can also help you manage inventory across multiple platforms.

OrderCup: OrderCup is a shipping and order management solution designed for e-commerce businesses, including Etsy. It automates order processing, label creation, and tracking. It also offers discounted shipping rates.

Aris Technologies: Aris Technologies offers Etsy shipping automation tools, including batch label printing and order syncing. It can streamline your order processing and label creation workflow.

When selecting a tool to automate order processing and label creation for your Etsy shop, consider your specific needs, the volume of orders you handle, and your preferred carriers. Many of these tools offer free trials, so you can test them to see which one best suits your business requirements. Additionally, check for any integration fees or subscription costs associated with the software.

All of these actions will help you scale your business. Start slowly and methodically, but make notes as you go. You'll find that some methods to scale your business are convenient at one time, and others at another. Keep your future file full! That gives you the best opportunity to seize the moment when you have some down time.

CHAPTER 10:
CUSTOMER
RETENTION

C ustomer retention is paramount in any business, and it holds particular significance for an Etsy business due to its direct impact on sustainability, growth, and profitability. There are plenty of reasons it's worth your attention, not the least of which is it is 7-15x more difficult and expensive to land a new customer than it is to retain an existing one! Here are some things customer retention does for you.

Profitability: Repeat customers are more likely to purchase higher-margin products or services and are less price-sensitive compared to new customers. Why? They trust you more and more with each purchase! Thus, they contribute more to the overall profitability of your business.

Word-of-Mouth Marketing: Satisfied and loyal customers are more likely to recommend a business to others, leading to positive word-of-mouth marketing and organic growth. They can even be persuaded to post on social media for you (with a link to your shop) and tag you if there is a discount to be had. This is great free advertising! Or gift a product to an influencer, and let them run wild! The more your customers post images of your products with happy stories and reviews, the better.

Brand Loyalty: Retaining customers builds brand loyalty, which insulates the business from competitive pressures. Loyal customers are less likely to switch to competitors solely based on price and are more forgiving of occasional hiccups in service. Also, they will see your newest offerings first, and become even more loyal over time!

Feedback and Improvement: Repeat customers provide valuable feedback that can be used to improve products, services, and overall customer experience. This feedback loop helps businesses stay relevant and competitive in the market. You may not always like what they have to say, but they have a vested interest in being honest with you: they want to buy more products!

Reduced Marketing Costs: Retaining customers requires less investment in marketing and advertising compared to acquiring new customers, leading to lower overall marketing costs. (More on this below.)

In an Etsy business, customer retention holds particular importance due to the platform's unique characteristics. Etsy shoppers aren't looking for a mass market product, they want something unique, and often personalized. That's part of the appeal of your particular shop – it resonates with your customers in a specific way. Overall, customer retention is vital for the sustained success of any business. It's extra important in an Etsy business due to the platform's emphasis on unique products, community engagement, and differentiation in a crowded marketplace.

Personalized Experience: Etsy is known for its emphasis on unique, handmade, and personalized products. Building long-term relationships with customers allows Etsy sellers to tailor their offerings to specific preferences and tastes, enhancing the overall customer experience.

Community and Connection: Etsy fosters a sense of community among buyers and sellers. Building relationships with customers goes beyond mere transactions; it involves creating meaningful connections and fostering a sense of belonging within the Etsy community. Buyers may follow you on multiple forms of social media, and even your blog! That creates a strong bond.

Differentiation in a Crowded Marketplace: Etsy is a highly competitive marketplace with thousands of sellers offering similar products. Customer retention strategies such as exceptional customer service, personalized communication, and loyalty programs can help sellers stand out amidst the competition and build a loyal customer base.

Repeat Purchases for Unique Items: Many Etsy products are one-of-a-kind or custom-made, making them suitable for repeat purchases. By retaining customers, Etsy sellers can capitalize on this aspect and encourage customers to return for future purchases or commissions.

Earning Repeat Business

There are many ways to ensure you maximize the possibility of earning repeat business. Here's a breakdown of various strategies for customer retention in an Etsy business.

Quality and Uniqueness

Etsy is home to millions of sellers offering a wide array of products. In such a crowded marketplace, product uniqueness is essential for standing out and attracting customers' attention. Unique products create a sense of exclusivity and appeal to customers seeking something special or one-of-a-kind. They are more likely to generate interest and drive repeat purchases from customers who value individuality and creativity.

High-quality products signal professionalism, craftsmanship, and attention to detail, enhancing customers' perception of value and trust in the brand. Positive experiences with quality products contribute to building a strong brand reputation and fostering customer loyalty. Satisfied customers are more likely to return for future purchases and recommend the brand to others.

Encourage Repeat Customers

Don't just sit back and hope it happens, encourage customers to shop with you multiple times. Strategies for encouraging repeat customers may include personalized recommendations, exclusive discounts or offers for returning customers, and maintaining high-quality products and customer service to ensure a positive experience. This involves addressing customers directly, both through your shop and through email.

In your shop, in a specific listing, if that product pairs well with another one, mention it! If these earrings match that necklace, say so! If this moisturizer has the same scent as that hand cream, point it out!

Capture and Use Contact Information

Collecting contact information, such as email addresses, allows Etsy sellers to maintain direct communication with customers beyond the initial purchase. You want to keep a record of everyone who has ever purchased from you for future email campaigns.

This information can be utilized for targeted marketing campaigns, such as email newsletters, promotions, or product updates, to re-engage past customers and encourage repeat purchases. These campaigns are highly effective when used sparingly, less than 7 per year. Choose your dates and topics wisely! Don't spam anyone's email with constant reminders of your shop; instead, carefully curate an email featuring products that are related to products they have purchased in the past, or are aligned with an upcoming holiday or occasion.

Make sure to set up a unique email address for your Etsy business so you're not sharing your personal contact information with your Etsy customers. No matter how nice they are, you want to maintain some personal privacy!

Follow Up with Customers

Following up with customers post-purchase demonstrates care and appreciation, fostering a sense of loyalty and goodwill. Ask them how they like the product, or for pictures of it in use. If the photos are good, ask them to post on social media, and offer a slight discount for a future purchase.

Personalized follow-up messages expressing gratitude for their purchase, requesting feedback, or offering assistance can enhance the overall customer experience and increase the likelihood of future purchases.

Provide Ongoing Value to Your Customer Base

Continuously providing value to customers beyond the initial purchase is crucial for fostering long-term relationships and sustaining their interest. You can put this information in your shop, your blog, social media, or all three.

This can be achieved through various means, such as offering educational content related to products, providing after-sales support, or introducing new products or collections that cater to their evolving needs and preferences.

Build Loyalty Programs And Rewards

Setting up rewards programs for an Etsy shop is an effective strategy to incentivize repeat purchases, foster customer loyalty, and differentiate your brand from competitors. Loyalty programs and rewards incentivize repeat purchases by offering customers tangible benefits or discounts for their continued patronage. Make these discounts time sensitive to encourage a sense of urgency. A coupon that is good for 60 days is more motivating than an open ended discount.

Etsy sellers can create loyalty programs that reward customers based on factors such as purchase frequency, total spending, or referrals, thereby fostering a sense of exclusivity and appreciation among loyal customers. Consider what type of loyalty program makes sense for you!

Here are some popular rewards program types.

Points-Based Rewards Program

Determine the actions that earn points. Decide which actions will earn customers points, such as making a purchase, leaving a review, or referring a friend.

Assign point values. Assign point values to each action based on its significance to your business. For example, a purchase might earn 1 point for every $10 spent, while referring a friend might earn 5 points.

Set redemption thresholds. Determine how many points customers need to accumulate before they can redeem them for rewards. Common thresholds include 100 points for a $5 discount or 500 points for a free product.

Communicate the program: Clearly explain your points-based rewards program on your Etsy shop's homepage, product listings, and checkout page. Consider creating a dedicated page outlining the program's details and terms. Check out other shops and see how they have listed their programs. Copy a style you like.

Tiered Loyalty Program

Define loyalty tiers. Create different tiers based on customer spending or engagement levels, such as Bronze, Silver, Gold, and Platinum.

Determine different tier benefits. Assign exclusive benefits to each tier, such as percentage discounts, free shipping, early access to new products, or personalized gifts. Each tier's benefits usually include the benefits from the tier below.

Establish qualification criteria. Specify the criteria customers must meet to reach each tier, such as total spending over a certain period or the number of purchases made.

Promote advancement. Encourage customers to progress to higher tiers by highlighting the benefits they can unlock and providing incentives to reach the next tier.

Referral Program

Define referral rewards. Decide what rewards both the referrer and the referred customer will receive. For example, offer a free gift, discount, or store credit to both parties.

Create unique referral links or codes. Generate unique referral links or codes for each customer to share with their friends and family. This allows you to track who did the referring.

Automate tracking. Use Etsy's messaging system or third-party tools to track referrals and attribute rewards accurately. A popular software is OSI Affiliate Software. Ask others in your niche which software they use, and check it out.

Promote the program. Encourage customers to refer friends by promoting the referral program through email newsletters, social media posts, and on your Etsy shop's homepage.

VIP Membership Program

Define VIP benefits: Determine the exclusive benefits VIP members will receive, such as early access to sales, special promotions, or personalized discounts.

Set membership criteria: Establish the criteria customers must meet to qualify for VIP membership, such as total spending over a certain period or the number of purchases made.

Communicate VIP perks: Clearly communicate the benefits of VIP membership and how customers can qualify on your Etsy shop's homepage, product listings, and checkout page.

Provide ongoing value: Continuously engage VIP members with exclusive offers, personalized recommendations, and VIP-only events to reinforce their loyalty and encourage repeat purchases.

When setting up rewards programs for your Etsy shop, it's essential to keep your customers' preferences and behaviors in mind. Tailor your programs to align with your brand identity and values, and regularly evaluate their effectiveness to make adjustments as needed. What works for one target audience may not be a great for another. By implementing rewards programs effectively, you can cultivate a loyal customer base and drive sustained growth for your Etsy business.

Customer retention in an Etsy business is not just about securing one-time transactions but about nurturing lasting relationships with customers. By implementing strategies such as encouraging repeat purchases, capturing contact information, following up with customers, building loyalty programs, and providing ongoing value, Etsy sellers can cultivate a loyal customer base that drives sustained business growth and success.

CHAPTER 11:
MOTIVATION AND
BURNOUT

Experiencing burnout at work can be incredibly challenging, both mentally and physically. In a creative endeavor like running an Etsy shop, it can come in many flavors, like "No Creativity Sauce" or "Burnout Hot Wings." I've been there! And I've come out of it. Knowing it passes helped me the second time around. Let's talk about both types of issues, and strategize a little around how to keep your attitude and your art fresh.

Generalized Shopkeeper Burnout

It's like hitting a wall of exhaustion and disillusionment, where the once fulfilling aspects of your job become overwhelming and draining. Turning on your computer can feel like turning on your "sad" button.

Burnout often results from prolonged stress, excessive workload, lack of control over tasks, and a feeling of not being recognized or appreciated for your efforts. Customers get on your last nerve. Slow periods feel like they will never end. The number of details to deal with seems endless, and you just don't want to do it!

Mentally, burnout can lead to feelings of apathy, cynicism, and a sense of detachment from your work. You might find it difficult to concentrate, make decisions, or muster up enthusiasm for tasks that used to interest you. Physically, you may experience fatigue, headaches, muscle tension, and difficulty sleeping as your body reacts to prolonged stress. You may dream of yelling at the customer who gave you a bad review, or running off and joining the circus.

To combat burnout and maintain a positive mood and focus, it's crucial to prioritize self-care and implement strategies to manage stress effectively. You need to start doing this *before you're at the end of your rope!* Unfortunately, once you're stressed out, it's harder to do, but better late than never.

Try These Steps To Keep Burnout At Bay

Set boundaries: Establish clear boundaries between work and personal life to prevent overworking and allow yourself time to recharge outside of work hours. Seriously, in your off hours, don't look at your work accounts online at all. At all! You need a break, and that includes your phone, your computer, and your tablet. Just be in your life – stay out of work when it's your personal time. Enjoy people, pets, places, and experiences. Work will still be there when you return.

Take breaks: Incorporate regular breaks throughout your workday to rest and recharge. Even short breaks can help alleviate stress and improve focus. I personally take 10-15 minutes every two hours, and whenever possible, spend those minutes moving. I'll go outside, or go up and down the hall or the stairs. Sometimes I take yoga breaks. Moving makes a huge difference. It moves your blood around, relaxes your body, encourages some deep breaths – in other words, it's good for you!

Practice mindfulness: Engage in mindfulness techniques such as deep breathing, meditation, or yoga to reduce stress and increase mental clarity. The goal is to literaly relax your brain for a few minutes. Not into meditation or yoga? Listen to music, dance, or engage in sports. Play with your pet! All have similar effects on the brain.

Seek support: Reach out to colleagues, friends, or a professional counselor for support and guidance. Use the Etsy Forums to talk to other shop owners. Talking about your feelings can help alleviate stress and provide perspective. Talk about good feelings and bad – they all matter! And it's great when other sellers can validate your experience. They may have creative ideas to help you streamline a challenging process.

Prioritize tasks: Break down your workload into smaller, manageable tasks and prioritize them based on importance and deadlines. Sometimes it's easy to look at all you want to accomplish and get overwhelmed. Focus on completing one task at a time to avoid that feeling. Crossing things off a list makes it easier to see when you're making progress.

Delegate when possible: If you have the option, delegate tasks to someone else, or ask for help when needed. I've listed several ways to automate processes here in this book, and I'm sure there are more I haven't thought of. Ask for help, and talk to other shopkeepers. Read blogs! There are great ideas out there.

Engage in hobbies: Make time for activities outside of work that bring you joy and fulfillment. Engaging in hobbies or interests can help reduce stress and improve your overall well-being. Even chatting with friends can bring your stress levels down. Make time to do what you love, and what feeds your soul. It matters!

Take care of your physical health:

Maintain a healthy lifestyle by eating nutritious foods, exercising regularly, and getting enough sleep. Physical health plays a significant role in managing stress and preventing burnout. The healthier you are, the less stress affects you.

But What If It's Creative Block?

Experiencing a creative block as an artist can be deeply frustrating and disheartening. It's like hitting a wall where your ideas suddenly seem stale, your creativity feels drained, and your usual flow of inspiration comes to a screeching halt. For me, I hate every piece of work I create – even if others like it, I can't stand it. It really stinks, but it passes! I promise!

When it's happening, it's as if you're in a mental fog where the clarity and excitement you usually feel about your work are replaced by a sense of stagnation and doubt.

Physically, it might manifest as a feeling of heaviness or tension in your mind, as if your thoughts are stuck in a loop, unable to break free and generate new ideas. Emotionally, it can lead to feelings of anxiety, self-doubt, and even a sense of loss or emptiness, particularly if creating art is a significant part of your identity and source of fulfillment. Sometimes it manifests as irritability as you try to create, and you just can't find a way to express what you're trying to do creatively.

As an artist, running low on inspiration or execution can make you question your abilities and purpose. You might find yourself staring at a blank canvas or screen, grappling with a sense of inadequacy or fear of failure. The pressure to produce something meaningful or innovative can intensify, adding to the mental blockage.

In essence, creative block feels like being trapped in a cycle of unproductivity and self-criticism, where the harder you try to force inspiration, the more elusive it becomes. However, it's essential to remember that creative blocks are a natural part of the creative process and often temporary. Finding ways to navigate through them, whether through taking a break, seeking inspiration from different sources, or experimenting with new techniques, can help reignite your creative spark and break through the blockage.

Strategies To Avoid Creative Block

Rotate Projects: Keep your creative juices flowing by rotating between different projects or product lines. This prevents burnout by allowing you to shift focus and maintain enthusiasm. If your shop curates digital or drop shipped items, focus on those for a few days or a week. It will help you bounce back.

Set Boundaries: Establish clear boundaries between work and personal time to prevent creative fatigue. Schedule regular breaks and downtime to recharge and rejuvenate. Just like shopkeeper burnout, you need to give the creative part of your brain rest, too!

Collaborate and Network: Collaborate with other artists or makers in real life, or within the Etsy community to exchange ideas, gain fresh perspectives, and reignite inspiration. Sometimes looking at someone's beautiful idea will spark something; sometimes looking at someone's terrible work will set me off in a good direction. You never know where inspiration lies, or when the head-clearing moment will come! Other artists are often the spark I need to get back on track.

Continuous Learning: Invest in your skills and knowledge through workshops, courses, or attending industry events to stay motivated and continuously improve your craft. Learning a new technique, or refreshing an old one, uses a different part of your brain than your primary creativity. It can help you gain perspective.

Listen to Feedback: Solicit feedback from customers, peers, and mentors to identify areas for improvement and ensure your products meet or exceed customer expectations. Happy customers are very motivating, but sometimes unhappy ones can be, too. Feedback can push you in a new direction, or help you add nuance to your work.

Experience a Different Art: If you're a visual artist, immerse yourself in music. A woodworker? Visit a museum. Digital artist? Go see a play, or a ballet recital. Different arts stimulate different parts of the creative brain. You'll open up your creative senses to receiving art, and you may find the inspiration you're looking for.

Do Creative Exercises: Experiment with creative exercises such as brainstorming, sketching, journaling, or mind mapping to stimulate ideas and overcome mental blocks.

Embrace Imperfection: Allow yourself to embrace

imperfection. Since perfection is unattainable, perfectionism can really zap your creative spirit. Sometimes imperfections are what make the art relatable. Sometimes they can lead us into a new design. Is there anything you can learn from this mistake? Is this imperfection beautiful in some way? Focus on progress rather than perfection and give yourself permission to explore and make mistakes.

Incorporating New Ideas And Innovation

Once you have reignited your desire to create and do business, you need to incorporate your new ideas into your work. A few ideas on that:

Don't rush in! Play with your ideas first, and make friends with them before you commit to making money with them. Some ideas and techniques grow quickly. Before you commit to a specific product or project, play with your ideas for a while to ensure that you acquire the materials you need for your best ideas.

Not every idea is a money maker. That's ok! Creativity doesn't always work that way. Play with the new idea anyway. Let it take you where it needs to take you.

Experiment: Embrace experimentation and exploration in your creative process by trying new materials, techniques, or design concepts. Don't be afraid to push boundaries and think outside the box. You may be on your way to something innovative, or you may be creating a genre defining nuance. Every experiment could result in a learning experience, or a new product line.

Research trends: Stay informed about industry trends, consumer preferences, and emerging technologies to identify opportunities for innovation and differentiation.

Introduce your innovations slowly if they are significantly different from your established brand. Your customers follow you for a reason: they like your brand. If you deviate from your norm too far too quickly, you'll lose customers. Go more slowly, and bring them with you.

Listen to customer feedback and incorporate suggestions or requests into your product development process to meet evolving needs and preferences.

Staying Relevant

Art that isn't evolving is dead. You need to keep evolving your perspective to keep your shop fresh and your customers engaged. How? By feeding your creativity and inspiration.

Curate inspiration boards: Create digital or physical inspiration boards featuring images, colors, textures, and themes that resonate with your brand aesthetic and inspire your creative process. Make one for any creative idea or product you're dreaming up – all your options and good ideas will live in one place.

Cross-pollinate the new with the old: Draw inspiration from diverse sources such as art, nature, travel, film, dance, or cultural influences to infuse fresh perspectives and creativity into your work. Blend disparate sources together to generate a new mood, shape, or image. Incorporate these new ideas into your existing products or themes.

Stay curious: Cultivate a curious mindset and remain open to new ideas, experiences, and inspiration from unexpected sources. Creativity hides in plain sight, but if you're not curious, you won't uncover it!

Explore other platforms: Explore social media platforms, design blogs, magazines, film, other websites, and art exhibitions to discover new artists, trends, and creative techniques that can inspire your work.

Engage with community: Participate in Etsy Forums, online communities, or local maker meetups to connect with fellow creatives, share ideas, and gain inspiration from their experiences. Go to an art fair, a museum shop, or an antique show with a focus on "How did they do that?"

Staying relevant is as much about what you do as what you don't do. The only way to do it is to stay immersed in artistic expression, and follow what stimulates you. If nothing is exciting to you, follow someone else's passion for a few days until yours returns. But stay active in art!

Slow Sales Periods

Every sales professional knows slumps happen. So does every athlete, performer, etc. And yet, when it happens to us, none of us can believe it's just a slump. We begin to doubt everything, and may get a heavy case of imposter syndrome.

Maybe it's them. Maybe it isn't you. Maybe the customer base just zigged when you zagged for a few weeks. No worries. It happens. They'll be back.

Maybe it's you. Use slow sales periods as an opportunity to reflect on your business goals, review your product offerings, and identify areas for improvement or innovation. Did you change things too much or too fast? Are your products high quality? How are your listings? Are they engaging? How are the photos? If you see that your quality or engagement is falling off, fix it!

Expand your product range or introduce seasonal offerings to attract new customers and generate interest during slower sales periods. Different times of year are quiet in different markets. If you know a slow one is coming, plan some really attractive items to drop just ahead of time!

Increase your marketing efforts through social media campaigns, email newsletters, collaborations, or special promotions to drive traffic to your Etsy shop and boost sales.

The fact is the market doesn't always find you on their own. Sometimes they need some reminding of how great you are. Marketing is the answer.

Enjoy the lull! If you can predict your quite time, that's a great time to take a few days off, or otherwise use the time wisely. You can focus on improving your craft, refining your product photography, updating your shop layout, or optimizing your listings to enhance the overall shopping experience for customers.

At some point, you're going to have some feelings of burnout or creative block. Use the strategies here to stay fresh, and keep those feelings at bay. When they come, realize they aren't permanent, and don't be too hard on yourself. Be patient, work the strategies, and then get back to work.

EPILOGUE

Congratulations on reaching the end of this comprehensive guide on starting and running an Etsy business! As you reflect on the wealth of knowledge and insights gained throughout this journey, remember that your success is within reach.

Starting an Etsy business is not just about selling products; it's about crafting a unique story, building meaningful connections with customers, and embarking on a fulfilling entrepreneurial adventure. Whether you're a seasoned artisan or a newcomer to the world of e-commerce, the principles outlined in this book serve as a roadmap to guide you through every step of the process.

As you venture forth into the world of Etsy entrepreneurship, keep in mind the following key takeaways:

Embrace Your Creativity: Your creativity is your greatest asset. Let it shine through in every aspect of your business, from product design and branding to customer interactions and marketing strategies. Embrace experimentation, stay true to your vision, and don't be afraid to think outside the box.

Prioritize Quality and Authenticity: In a marketplace saturated with mass-produced goods, quality and authenticity are your greatest allies. Focus on creating products that are impeccably crafted, uniquely designed, and infused with your personal touch. Strive to deliver an exceptional customer experience that sets you apart from the competition.

Build Relationships, Not Just Transactions: Etsy is more than just a platform for buying and selling; it's a community of like-minded individuals united by a passion for creativity and craftsmanship. Take the time to build genuine relationships with your customers, fellow sellers, and supporters. Engage with your audience authentically, listen to their feedback, and show appreciation for their support.

Embrace Continuous Learning and Growth: The journey of entrepreneurship is filled with ups and downs, successes and setbacks. Embrace every challenge as an opportunity for growth and learning. Stay curious, stay adaptable, and stay committed to your vision. Invest in your personal and professional development, seek out mentorship and support, and never stop striving for excellence.

Celebrate Your Successes: Along the way, remember to celebrate your successes, both big and small. Every sale, every positive review, and every milestone achieved is a testament to your hard work, dedication, and perseverance. Take pride in how far you've come and use each success as fuel to propel you forward toward even greater heights.

Take Care of Yourself: Working a side hustle doesn't mean working yourself into the ground. Pace yourself! Your first year is as much of a learning experience as it is a business venture. Take time to do things you love, spend time relaxing, and remember to take breaks. Self-care is good for business, and for you.

As you turn the final page of this book and embark on your Etsy journey, know that the possibilities are endless. With passion, persistence, and a commitment to excellence, you have the power to turn your dreams into reality and create a thriving Etsy business that brings joy, fulfillment, and prosperity to your life and the lives of others.

So go forth with confidence, creativity, and courage, and may your Etsy business journey be filled with boundless success, happiness, and inspiration. Remember, the world is waiting to be enchanted by what you have to offer. Embrace the adventure, embrace the possibilities, and embrace the extraordinary journey that lies ahead.

www.ingramcontent.com/pod-product-compliance
Lightning Source LLC
Chambersburg PA
CBHW072247310526
45795CB00011B/279